JOURNEY TO YOUR SUMMIT

JOURNEY TO YOUR
SUMMIT

Intersection of Life Planning and
Financial Literacy with a Spiritual
and Disciplined Focus

DAVE VETTA

Palmetto Publishing Group
Charleston, SC

Journey to Your Summit
Copyright © 2020 by Dave Vetta
All rights reserved

First Edition

Printed in the United States

ISBN-13: 978-1-64111-830-9
ISBN-10: 1-64111-830-X

CONTENTS

DEDICATION

Katy Vetta

David, Johnny, and Kate Williams; Ava and Capri Maycock

Sara and Mike Maycock; Annie and Joe Williams; Kelsey and

Geoff Rowe

Purpose and Prologue

Through a career in investments, finance, planning, and working with countless high-net-worth individuals, crystalizing their goals and strategies to accomplish them; I chose the purpose statement, "Journey to your summit." First of all, it's very difficult to get somewhere if you're not sure where it is you are going, even if you are making good time (and busy as all get-out). Once you determine your goals and objectives (your summit), there is the "how to" accomplish them—the strategies, tactics, execution, adjusting, and remaining on course.

Much time should first be spent on why these are your goals, how committed you are to them, refining them, and very likely putting some plans in place as you formulate your goals and stoke your passion.

So, while I continue to learn, grow, observe, and evolve, I have been heading down this path for some time, intrigued by human behavior, development, motivation, leadership and results.

This is about life planning, which is broad, multifaceted, and often a little bit vague when getting started, so there are certified life coaches and certified financial planners, with the latter focusing more on financial resources, habits, and outcomes.

Financial planning may appear an easier default from life planning because of formulas, processes, absolute math, and more tangible milestones. Historically, it is easier to frame a conversation around these. There are some who have combined financial and life planning (i.e., Mitch Anthony, George Kinder, and others). The two are inextricably linked for happiness and fulfillment, which is simply aligning resources, financial and otherwise, with priorities and goals. So this will underscore this work: your *why* of life financial planning, your *how* steps, and your ability to stay on track.

There will be two subthemes that I found prevalent misnomers in some respects (and they are often public defaults), yet they are essential ingredients to the fulfillment and achievement of your hopes and dreams. First, some degree of financial literacy can contribute significantly to your satisfaction, helping you to realize your dreams and feel that you have the ability to influence or control some tangible outcomes. Even if you disavow all material things and seek your summit, it is hard to escape someone or something without financial consequences, requirements, and the ability to eat and survive. Basic literacy is the ability to read and write, while the broader definition is competency or knowledge in a specific area. Financial literacy is how money works and, more importantly, how it can work for you.

Second, another often pursued, misunderstood, or ignored concept is retirement planning. People are ill prepared or unsure of how and where to start. I was going to title this book *Retirement States You're Heading For: Confusion and Denial.* Many I have seen or heard of are in this state of denial. "I will sell my business, receive inheritance or government help, my partner will handle it, and there is no need to think about any other aspect other than. I can't wait to turn sixty-two and do nothing" is what they say. Sound enticing? You might be retired for thirty years, or maybe your partner has other plans, or what if your plan doesn't materialize? Therefore, accepting and embracing the need to do something earlier rather than later is *huge!*

That's where the other state, the state of confusion, may be where you are headed. Where do I start? What does it look like? How do I get there? How do I adjust when life diverts my path? Find a coach, find resources, align with professionals, get up the learning curve, be prepared to take a sabbatical, reinvent, redefine, and advance or grow your way to a fulfilling life experience.

When looking to those who have achieved success, fulfillment, and a legacy lasting multiple generations, I have found two prevailing contributors: 1) a spiritual focus (having strong faith in something at work that is larger than ourselves), and 2) militarylike precision and a discipline, being tested and thriving under adverse circumstances. While raised Catholic, but not being particularly religious, I have witnessed and grown to have a very healthy respect for people's different views on spirituality, intangible gifts, a strong faith in something higher, and conviction, which optimizes the human condition and spirit. It is the power of mind and body beyond our comprehension to achieve, survive, and care greatly.

With great respect for our military, veterans, and their families in the melding of life-and-death situations with processes and systems to help ensure some of the most promising outcomes, we have much to learn from our military. What may come to mind are negative examples or reasons not to think more of spirituality or mirroring elements from the military. Think about those best cases, those examples where spirituality and the military shine, and bring out the best in people. There will be a few real stories and positive examples later in this material. Often, stories of spirituality or military that are less than stellar lie in the messenger not the message. For example, the priest or minister may not communicate the right message in the right tone, or the officer in the military may not give the best example or delivery of sound principles. There are those who are strong in the faith of church ministry and operations of military discipline. That is different than the administrative work in the church or those levels in our country's department of defense. I say this to distinguish the message from the messenger, and the related circumstances.

Life's lessons in leadership, principled methods, surviving adversity, teamwork, and unity are not without challenges, but talking about a sense of higher purpose, a greater sense than yourself, the giving of your life to God and/or country—these are all solid foundations for success and fulfillment.

Sharpened Number 2 Lead Pencil: Ongoing Therapy

I have always felt comfortable, smarter, and wiser with a sharpened number 2 lead pencil in my hand and a supply at the ready. Too many standardized tests or blue-book exams, I guess (those didn't always end well, by the way).

Many lead pencils have been destroyed by my note-taking, planning pieces, numbers, and observations over the years. This book started as self-therapy, learning, processing, and refining. The following are some of the results of that process, but it is an ongoing process for all of us. At every turn, the premise and purpose of these contents have been reinforced and have stood the test of time.

There is a small part of me that thinks with humility that I have learned some things from the thousands of people with whom I have interacted over the years that have value to some and will add value as time goes on for them. At the heart of my mission and my identity is supporting people in journeying to their summits, and discovering and reaching their ultimate goals.

For some, it's being prepared financially; for some, it's all the other planning, but mostly pulling the trigger and taking some calculated risks when the planning is done and recognizing opportunities along the way.

It's often not about the money. Over the years, I have had the good fortune of working with many successful people as we might define them by their business, financial resources, material things, social circle, family, and friends.

A surprisingly high number of materially successful people defined by the trappings were ill prepared or not happy or satisfied when their businesses were sold, as they tried to define their success outside the business financial statements, nor did they think about preserving, perpetuating, and transitioning their business. They are entrepreneurs with an idea, a skill, and a passion—and good for them. They have achieved financial success beyond the dreams of many, but were not happy, fulfilled, or worry free.

Initiatives and Underlying Themes

With this in mind, it poses the question: What does retirement mean to you? It may not simply mean work to sixty-five and move to some golf course to take on your golf handicap. Retirement, sabbaticals, or extended leaves are multidimensional, and they are happening earlier and earlier—voluntarily or involuntarily.

Many equate financial security with a happy retirement. This is one piece of it, and not necessarily the most important piece. This book focuses primarily on the nonfinancial ingredients of a fulfilling advancement, and also identifies a number of essential elements of the financial piece.

Retirement does not have to be downshifting or slowing down, just changing lanes. To have a happy, successful, and productive retirement, you need to prepare in your thirties, forties, fifties, sixties, and beyond. Productive and meaningful contributions will take different forms, but do not need to stop with age.

Even *Webster*'s definition of retirement is outdated: "withdrawal from work, business etc. because of age." This is a misnomer and a debilitating definition. Advancement means "to bring closer to the present, to go forward, move ahead, to make progress, improve, develop to use in rank and importance; moving toward an objective." Obtain a proper focus on the evolution of advancement; build skill sets, interests, contacts, relationships, and, yes, your bank account. Happy and healthy retirement or advancement is not reserved for the affluent. Said another way, being affluent does not ensure a happy and healthy retirement.

There will be challenges and impediments all along the way. Take responsibility now for a happy and healthy *advancement!* Don't waste time blaming others for being where you are at or having some elements of unpreparedness. Get rid of the guilt and blame for not doing more sooner or making some mistakes. List the things in your way, and address them.

———

What makes you young at heart? Each of us is in need of others to depend on for support and encouragement. Select, consciously, friends, coworkers, and certain family members who are positive and supportive, with similar values and objectives. This circle of influence can make a lot of difference in a happy and healthy retirement. Constantly revalidate spiritual beliefs and values. Seek perspective with which to grow and thrive. Once you deal with your mortality, you will focus on living, not dying.

In the movie *It's a Wonderful Life*, a perennial Christmas favorite, Jimmy Stewart and Donna Reed are playfully walking home after falling in the high school pool at a school dance and are inadvertently being observed by an older man. When Jimmy talks about kissing Donna Reed and does not do it, the old man exclaims that "youth is wasted on the young." This strikes me as being similar to many individuals who have some degree of affluence but are not satisfied; they are not sure of their goals and how much money is enough to accomplish them. They compare themselves to others, creating a constant state of frustration, rather than benchmarking against their own objectives and dreams. Money can be wasted on the affluent.

In thirty-plus years of working with affluent individuals, I am most impressed with the drive, determination, and success of many. Also, I am surprised that once they have financially achieved beyond what they thought possible, they are ill prepared to deal with it; they are not happy and not sure what to do about it. Money was the end and not necessarily the means to the end.

You must consistently apply sound financial *principles* that guide this process. I have spent much of my career working with people to aid in the implementation of these financial strategies, given that there are a few moving parts, such as setting financial targets, putting in place a sound investment program, and generating sufficient income through jobs, investment income, risk management, disciplined spending, and *time*.

You are not alone in not having the answers to a lot of questions. These next pages may provide some answers to help you focus on what is most helpful to you as you seek a rewarding, fulfilling, and exciting experience through all phases of life—especially that of advancement, which you have worked (and are continuing to work) hard to fulfill by picking up this book.

Perhaps you or someone you know has won the lottery, or maybe you have dreams of winning. It is interesting that those who do win often are struggling, and not long after winning, have gone through most of their windfall. What's missing is a well-grounded discipline and balanced approach to life, which makes the lifestyle sustainable. Money was the end, and when it was obtained, they quit their jobs, and there was not a clear sense of purpose and objectives. Therefore, it is not unusual to find oneself in a financial tailspin.

Working and contributing are lifetime needs and activities. This is the process of giving back—zeroing in on a sense of purpose and a sense of fulfillment. Evidence of this is encouraging, exciting, and promising for continued growth in our society and economy, as well as growth and contributions to charitable causes. I've worked with many people who will worry about money, whether they have a dollar and a quarter in the bank, or $1.25 million. Know your ingredients of happiness and fulfillment.

Some concerns and primary objectives for people are first seeking security through financial safety nets. Define this, and you will have a much better chance of attaining these goals. Many people today are forced to deal with retirement due to a layoff or significant change at one's place of employment. This can be like falling off a cliff. The bottom falls out, and they are not prepared whatsoever. Layoffs are more a part of life today than ever. Chances are, it will happen to you and me. Consider the possibility, and plan accordingly.

The human psychology of having financial means, how one acquires money, and what plans one has to spend it on are important. I know of good people who have found themselves with significant sums of money, due to an inheritance or the sale of business, who become depressed about having wealth and what they would now do to achieve a sense of purpose and self-esteem.

This was really an adjustment for these people in their thirties and forties. You may say that it would be different in their fifties and sixties, and I believe it is the same issue: that older people may be no more prepared for advancement. Some do not know how to invest and preserve capital, as this may contribute to the angst as well. Being frightened of the unknown and of uncertainty can contribute to anxiety.

Having raised some concerns and how you might address them, I must also say that no one has all the answers as you approach advancement. Know yourself, set boundaries, set out on the course, make adjustments, and keep moving forward. Hopefully, the pages of this book can accelerate the learning process so you can prepare for or continue in your retirement years.

Inspect what others are doing to prepare for retirement only after you, or you and your significant other, have determined some boundaries. Otherwise, you will be reacting and missing the target. When you follow the aforementioned sequence for planning and preparation, this will result in sustainable confidence, commitment, and passion. Have courage and self-respect to dream, and be committed to seeing your dreams come true.

———

When our kids were small, my wife, Katy, and I played for them a recording by Bob Mowat, which offered some positive ideas for kids on approaching life. Mr. Mowat offered that if something is worth doing, it's worth doing badly at first. Just like you will likely take on things that you are not good at but have an acute interest in—maybe carpentry, piano lessons, flying lessons, yoga—financial literacy shouldn't be discouraging but should be a commitment nurtured by determination.

Biography: Why Me?

Having enough psychology courses to earn a minor in college (and probably be dangerous), along with a business major in undergraduate studies and an MBA with an emphasis in organization and development, I spent time running human resources, marketing, and immersion in leadership development at the University of Virginia Darden School of Business, and I was a guest lecturer at University Systems in Wisconsin on finance and leadership. I also worked directly with hundreds of investment and private banking clients, business owners, CEOs, community leaders, and institutional leaders, and I have spoken in front of many on careers, leadership, finance, community, and service. I did this while maintaining a certified financial planning designation for over twenty years.

I was fortunate to have been recognized by industry, community, leadership, and philanthropic organizations. But most importantly, I possess a desire to contribute, a curiosity, and a belief that we all can learn from one another and achieve amazing results.

At this point in life, maybe you are committed to achieving your dreams and aspirations, not someone else's. Crystalize and harvest those dreams. Take the first step—that is the hardest—and keep going, adapting along the way. People who seem to have it all together work on it every day, so let's begin the *journey to your summit.*

CHAPTER 1

Prepare Now with an Eye on the Future

The future is something which everyone reaches
at the rate of 60 minutes an hour.
—C. S. Lewis

Keeping one eye on the future and one eye on the present may leave you cross-eyed, but it doesn't have to. Dream about your future, and take small steps to get closer to it. Some are consumed by a dream, working very hard to make it happen, and the savings required to realize it.

Enjoy the moment each day, be present as much as you can, and be grateful for the lessons and experience of the past, but don't be retirement poor (where you don't have enough disposable income to truly enjoy the now). Educate yourself and establish a lifestyle that brings quality and satisfaction to your life. Be open to opportunities, callings, and new and exciting paths while you commit to the dreams you have now.

What may seem to be mysteriously overwhelming is to create or begin to build a legacy as some of these accomplished lives you read about. If you do something consistently for long enough, you will look back and be amazed at your achievements. It may be an academic course that, over time, results in a degree, a part-time job, regular volunteering, or working on a house or car that leads to amazing results.

Many think about it, but most do not initiate it, and of those that do, most quit doing it along the way. Allow yourself some simple positive reinforcement and reassurance regularly that this is still the right path and one that you will be proud to look back on. A little discipline goes a long way. Take a small step and repeat; think about how satisfying it will be when completed. Build habits into your life, and one of them may be to take time to relax and recharge. Sometimes it's OK to do nothing, revalidate what's important, and make a little progress each day. You'll get tired, wander, and question whether it's the right path, but keep moving forward to new heights and awareness. The evolution of what you are working on will likely supersede the exercise of always seeking your perfect passion on a grand scale.

Add building blocks each day to get you closer to being the best and building your dream. Don't let a sin of omission give you a sense of guilt or regret. Many think of what they didn't do or get done and wish they had; instead, keep the prize in sight, stick with it, check out the competitive landscape of the relevance of your dream, and adapt. Embrace life's challenges and disruptions, and keep on track. We had a neighbor some time back who was a medical doctor, an accomplished musician (writing his own music), and an experienced pilot. It didn't just happen; he worked at it, refined goals and priorities, worked hard, and made sacrifices. Make conscious decisions, and when life happens, you can keep moving ahead.

The following passages are a few vignettes, stories, and observations of others that might resonate with you.

My Passion, or Yours?

I never quite thought about it like this, but a dear friend of mine, a career veteran of the navy, a helicopter pilot, a veteran of the technology field, and active philanthropist, made the comment that he wished he would have pursued his passion and purpose at a much younger age. This surprised me, as he seemingly embraces life with boundless energy and enthusiasm. As I reminded him of this and all he had accomplished and contributed, he said, "Yes, but I made others' passion my passion, not the other way around." Well, I still think he is remarkable, and it is as admirable to embrace what you are doing as if it were your own idea and resource.

Part of the point of this is that you may very well be better prepared to advance through life's stages if you invest time early on seeking, finding, and pursuing your purpose and passion. Take inventory, make mistakes, acquire credentials and experience, zero in, eliminate many, and give it a try. You may have more resiliency and rebound ability when in your twenties and thirties. If you believe there aren't that many original ideas, craft your version, convert it to your own, and commit!

This is another perspective and reason retirement planning, financial and otherwise, starts in your twenties and thirties. Having said all that, it may take it to another level if you organically discover and feed your personal passion and purpose. My friend is seeking that in his sixties, but this is OK because he is embracing life each day—I'm not sure it really matters who started it, but it is what you do with it!

A Week Facilitating Vacation Bible School: The Teacher Becomes the Student

We hear a lot about what motivates millennials, baby boomers, or Gen Xers—I would tell you that all you need to know for all these artificial age categories you can learn by spending time with three-, four-, and five-year-olds in an organized setting. In this case, I was the not-so-able assistant to my wife Katy, who facilitated Vacation Bible School for a week. Here is what I learned on this journey:

Katy is an experienced kindergarten teacher. She told me that most of the time, she is trying to figure out how each of her former students was different, and what made them tick. So, while activities and keeping them busy are important, it's more important to determine what motivates them, where they're coming from, and to individualize your approach considering their social, economic, and parental influences.

It was a fine line between manners and meltdowns. Determining what kind of day they were having (and whether you are close to either of these) is a gift and a challenge. Certainly, with a meltdown, you need to figure out what can bring them back to Mannerville, and that takes some thought. I can't say that I figured it out in a week, or that I am completely back from *my* meltdown!

Don't assume you know what is on their mind. Little Connor was working on his dance moves and his singing while the music was playing and we were on our second verse of "God Is Good." I was standing next to him and asked him how he was doing. Midstep, he looked at me thoughtfully and said, "I don't know if I have a red T-shirt at home that I need to wear to school tomorrow." Each day, we had a different T-shirt color to wear, and this was a morning where he was sporting an orange one. He had just arrived at school, was in the middle of an activity, and was worrying his little head over whether it was appropriate to wear his red hockey shirt the next day. It was very cute, and very much a surprise to me.

With a different day, there was a different mood—the first day, they were unfamiliar, uncertain, uncomfortable. They hadn't met us before and were a little nervous. In the ensuing days, they very quickly became familiar and comfortable with us and their nine other classmates, and began to trust and enjoy. Not every day was built on the prior though; some days, they took a setback, and we had to start over again, but the learning curve was quicker than day one and more productive. We would build on it and keep feeding the base of trust and support.

They were very much aware of right and wrong and whether they and others were being treated fairly and held accountable to the same standard. Long after class was done for the day, Ava informed me that her cousin cut in line in front of her, which was inappropriate at the time. Earlier in the day, I was informed by her cousin David, also in the class, that I was incorrectly telling Ava what her job was—that she pulled from a hat at the start of class and I did not understand that she was actually doing her job. Turned out he was right, and I was wrong, for which I apologized to the two five-year-olds (who also happened to be our grandchildren). Snack time is a very delicate time as well, as I was called out because someone that had more than their share of pretzels, oranges, and chocolate chips. Some may not have said anything, but they notice everything!

These are cute stories, but within them are real-life principles and values of respect, fairness, trust, and feeling appreciated for your opinion and what you contribute. These are recurring themes throughout these stories, observations, and real people and circumstances. So whether you are a manager, leader, or a student of life who is trying to understand people and relationships, check with the teachers these adults had years ago, and you can see where the die was cast!

If you can't locate their teachers, check out the Gospel of Matthew 18:3–4: "Truly I tell you, unless you change and become like children, you will never enter the kingdom of heaven. Whoever becomes humble like this child is the greatest in the kingdom of heaven." Or Matthew 11:25: "Although you have hidden these things from the wise and learned, you have revealed them to the childlike." Go ahead—it's OK to act like a kid now and then and bring out the child in all of us!

Build a Résumé—Then Burn It?

Does that make any sense? We are all wired differently, with varying degrees of drive and ambition and different scorecards. It strikes me that you work your whole professional career to learn skills, acquire credentials, and build relationships with family, clients, associates—and then you just stop? Don't get me wrong; relaxing and unplugging, going to a quiet spot and reading, meditating, praying, doing absolutely nothing, is great and essential. That time might be short lived or last a long time. The contrast, flexibility, and choices are awesome.

Find a platform or a jumping-off point for your sweet spot to leverage your talents and the things you really like to spend your time on. A wooden diving board has a foundation anchored in the ground and several planks, or a wooden bridge with a number of planks and lengths that traverse many a chasm. Keep those planks you want for your platform, and continue to build them in a new and deeper direction.

Maybe you have a myriad of hobbies for your growth. One of my hobbies is traveling, specifically checking out the US Supreme Court in session. While exploring this pastime and finding myself near Washington DC more often, I didn't even really think about the fact that this played into another goal of mine: visiting as many national parks as I can. Well, DC is one of the best officially designated national parks in our country. Pursue those hobbies. If you have many to tackle at once, that's great.

If you don't have hobbies and think it's too late to start, consider this quote by Cass Gilbert, architect of the Supreme Court building in DC. In 1929, as he learned that he was appointed to design the current building that houses our Supreme Court, he stated, "Thus, opens a new chapter in my career. And at 70 years of age I am now to undertake to carry through the most important and notable work of my life." He thought his work, career, and main interests were behind him. The best is yet to come—it's up to you!

Back to the Future

So here you are at a stage or chapter where you, or someone close to you, thinks you should be retiring or slowing down. Whether you do it or not is totally up to you and your partner—if you have a team.

The stereotypes of what you thought of your teachers, coaches, and parents in their fifties and sixties are alive and well. You will have people open the door for you, speak more slowly and loudly, and ask you if you know what an email is. Drives me nuts! But I digress…

It's natural to reflect, rewrite things, and maybe regret a little. OK, do it and get on with it. The only thing productive about looking back is if you are doing the family genealogy tree—it's not what you are leaving, but what you are moving on to. Where can you contribute, grow, be your best, and excel?

Mitch Anthony, an author and advisor to many financial consultants, calls it ROI, return on individual, or life-centered planning. Invest in yourself; it is possible to work a job, pursue your interests, and take all your vacation time. You will be glad you did as you look ahead. When you do this, you will look back with the purpose of creating the future you want, and that exit ramp will lead you to an exciting on-ramp! These are principles Mitch Anthony and his business partner, Steve Sanduski, teach to many financial advisors for their clients.

Supreme Power of Your Convictions

When you learn to tap into the world spiritually, results are beyond our human imagination. Whether you attribute to spirituality or not, please think about this and the real-life example that I am about to share.

You can read books like *Tipping Point*, *Nudge*, and *Butterfly Effect* to realize the tremendous influence you can have over time. There seem to be forces at work that we cannot account for in the outcomes that gain energy and dimension beyond human comprehension. It allows us to see the limitless extent of the human will.

As you grow, age, and evolve, it can be beneficial to find something you believe in and commit. This means something different to everyone, but we will all be amazed at the power, sustainability, and boundless dimensions to this over time. Conversely, there are a multitude of countless examples of people starting something but never finishing.

If you want an investment example, a mutual fund manager performing at median for one year, which is seemingly mediocre, over a five-year period could very well perform in the top quartile (the top 25 percent of comparable money managers). This is evidence of consistency—sticking to something. Many one-hit wonders fall by the wayside over time.

I can think of a most powerful example of longevity and depth of commitment to something that is right and this individual believes in. Soon after WWII, Ben Frenecz found himself a chief prosecutor at age twenty-seven at the Nuremberg trials beginning in 1947. Standing five feet tall, he supervised the process of bringing justice for the unimaginable atrocities committed in WWII. He turns one hundred this year and has never wavered in pursuing justice for those unable to help themselves. When asked why and how he could keep the fire burning for so long and with such vigor and zeal, he says, "Because it is the right thing to do." Please read more about him.

Maybe our passion and our purpose are at as high a life-defining and age-defying level as Mr. Frenecz, and maybe they're not; either way, find yours, and pursue it relentlessly because it is the right thing to do for you!

Believe It or Not

Financial and life planning are not often associated with spirituality; however, this was again validated for me. I was fortunate to spend some time with a senior, influential leader in the church. We were talking about his experience of melding business with ministry while commiserating over our golf game arranged by a dear friend.

According to this priest, at the heart of people reaching their goals and pulling themselves out of poverty is faith, a belief that anything is possible and that they have been given the talent to succeed. Simply put, if you don't believe in anything, it won't happen. Add a job, some education, and you are off and running. By the way, after our conversation and lunch, this friendly man of God very reverently reminded me I owed him ten dollars from our golf bet. I didn't think he cared about material things…

The point is, believe in something; why not a Higher Power who espouses good? Make the most of your gifts, be the best person you can be, and reach your goals—albeit maybe sometime on His schedule. Believe it, say it, and do it, for there is everything to gain.

People Who Seemingly Have It All Together Work on It Every Day

Financial security is one piece of it but it's not the most important piece. What are you chasing? What if you caught it?

Following are several attributes I have observed where people have stuck out positively. Their families seemed to have adopted these as well, and there appears to be a consistency in behaviors and outcomes:

- Advancement. Move toward an objective; go forward. Improve; make progress.
- Grounded principles, objectives, and plans. Take money out of equation.
- Spiritual enlightenment is essential to know the ultimate retirement.
- Deal with impediments—guilt, mortality. Use it or lose it.
- Once you deal with mortality, you will focus on living, not dying.
- Are you prepared to deal with success?

- Would you and your partner score similarly on retirement objectives?
- Working and contributing are lifetime needs and activities.
- Happiness is not determined by the size of the wallet.
- Inability to deal with mortality precludes many from dealing with wealth and estates.
- Have courage, conviction, and self-respect to dream and take action.

"We Are What We Believe We Are"

So, hopefully, part of the value I can bring is to be a conduit or distiller of things that I have learned from others. I am now taking time to note these things and am sure you are pretty busy doing other things. Part of this may be like a *Reader's Digest* condensed version and, as a good friend said, "worthy of underlining and incorporating." I put this in the category of quoting a few highly quotable resources.

A dear friend suggested a book, which I picked up, by C. S. Lewis. He's an amazing prolific author, historian, and communicator who helped folks through World War I and World War II with his books, broadcasts, and insights. Many can relate their experiences, but he says it in a few words. Some time ago, I remember someone once said they had written a book that was over five hundred pages long and it was suggested to them that it must've really taken a long time to write a book that long, to which she replied, "I didn't have enough time to write a shorter book." That struck me as to the challenge and gift to put complex stories and concepts simply. That's something that should be celebrated and cherished. With that in mind, the following are a few quotes attributed to C. S. Lewis:

> *You are never too old to set another goal or dream a new dream.*
> *The homemaker has the ultimate career, all other careers exist for one purpose only—and that is to support the ultimate career.*
> *Isn't it funny how day to day nothing changes, but when you look back, everything is different.*
> *Many view God as an airman views a parachute, it's there for emergencies, but they hope to never need it.*
> *True humility is not thinking less of yourself, it is thinking of yourself less.*

You will see these quotes placed in sections later on.

"To Be or Not to Be"

Throughout life in the Midwest, one looks for value and is rather frugal, even if you have the means. In fact, one may very well lead to the other. This decision is not so easy when it comes to accepting or admitting to eligibility for senior discounts. In fact, I think I saw a billboard that read, "Seniors have had their entire life to save for a cup of coffee; college kids and millennials really could use the discount!" Maybe so, but maybe it depends on the amount saved, and maybe there will be a sign.

I was minding my own business going through the McDonald's drive-through—the drive-through, mind you. It must've been a McDonald's I frequented, because when

I ordered my coffee through the intercom and pulled up to pay, she said that would be 95 cents for a senior coffee. As we pulled ahead, I complained to my wife next to me about the nerve of that worker to imply I fit the definition of a senior, which I guess McDonald's defines as over fifty-five. I must have gotten a little excited, because I drove right past the window to pick up my coffee and kept going, driving past my waiting coffee. I hadn't gone far when I realized, with my wife's gleeful help, I'd had a moment. I sheepishly went back and got my senior coffee. Arguably, I had my sign—ready or not. Others decide what you can or can't think, can or can't do, can or can't afford, if you let them. Don't let them! Relax. You made it, you qualify, sit back, and enjoy your coffee!

It's There if We Look!

Having interacted with, attended, and supported a number of universities at a variety of levels, there are a couple of facts that have always confused me.

First, it is not unusual for nearly 40 percent of first-year college freshman to drop out of school, or get side-tracked and leave for some time. Visiting a local university in Charleston, South Carolina, I noted that their suggested formula for advising students in successful graduation is the following:

- Establish goals.
- Be clear on options/courses.

- Identify values, strengths, interests, and abilities.
- Recognize challenges and competing demands.
- Develop action plans.
- Monitor with accountability.

I thought these had a broad application in life. Hopefully, you have or are working on some version of this for what you want in life.

The second statistic is that generally, fewer than 10 percent of college graduates support their alma mater financially—not just in the early years, but *ever*. This is not an indictment on universities or their graduates, but sort of a parallel with life: the emotional connection and engagement we feel throughout.

How many four-to-five-year periods in life, analogous to the time you spent at school, might you say have not built, fostered, or tapped into an emotional element or connection? Such that you are grateful for how it has influenced you and molded you, and you want to somehow show appreciation, pay back, or pay it forward for the years to come?

Candidly, I did not fully optimize the opportunities at the schools I attended; this was not their fault; it was mine. The overall experience was positive for me, and my family and friends and I grew to appreciate it, so I tapped into it and felt compelled to give back. My point is that there are many resources, kind and capable people, and opportunities presented to have you be what you want to be. It's there if we are looking for it!

Old Habits Die Hard

Why does it seem our happiness awareness index is on the rise, yet in people who are self-proclaimed to be happy, happiness is on the decline?

We think about happiness, measure it, tweet it, chase it, lament it when it's not there, and wonder where it went.

Defining happiness, success, contentment, and fulfillment is good but risky. What does it mean when we are not happy? Well, that's something only you can decide for yourself.

I once asked a dear friend how his ninety-four-year-old father woke up every day and seemed happy and content. So what does a ninety-four-year-old formula have to do with someone who is decades younger? Everything! It's a mindset, a way of life, a way of thinking, a way of talking, relating, and behaving. This may seem simple, but think about it. His father does the following:

- He realizes that he has what he wants and always wanted. He is not a rich man but is comfortable, and he lives in the home he raised his family in and lived in with his late wife until her recent passing.
- He has friendships. His late wife was his best friend, and she passed away three years ago. He talks over his day with her every evening, and he cared for her in her later years in that same home. Close friends, whether they are your partner or otherwise, who care for you and are good, kind people, will support you and be with you beyond measure.

- He is surrounded by family. They continually nurture and support him, and, while not perfect (as no family is), they are a nice reminder of the good life and work of his marriage. A strong sense of community, related or not, can contribute greatly.

- He has faith in God and himself. He believes in a good world, good people, and good outcomes, and he has had fewer health issues than some of his kids.

- He wakes up *grateful* every day.

- He's a creature of habit. A routine, a reliable schedule, consistent interdependence, are expectations that are met most days. Automatic pilot or muscle memory? I don't think so, but he has a body trained by a mind over years. Perseverance and habit go hand in hand and are both critical.

- He doesn't complain. I bet there are days he would love to and does, but they are rare, and he realizes it is of no value. Positive and constructive behaviors are outcomes of positive thoughts and words.

Frankly, I wish I would have thought about this when I was in my twenties and thirties and forties because it's true that old habits die hard—so it's much better if they are good habits.

SUMMARY AND ACTIVITY

Summary

- It's OK to act like a kid now and then and bring out the child in all of us.
- The best is yet to come; it's up to you to plan and motivate.
- Pursue your passions relentlessly, or discover your passions and work toward them.
- Remember: People who have it all together work on it every day. You can have it all together too.
- True humility is not thinking less of yourself; it is thinking of yourself less.

Activity

What does your future look like for you and your family? Be realistic in one column based on your current financial status, and your dream future in the second column.

Be honest about your status today. Where are you on this journey? Date it to look back on.

Date: _____

What are three things you can advance in your life to best close the gap?

1.
2.
3.

CHAPTER 2

Put Money in Its Place

We are what we believe we are.
—C. S. Lewis

We need to talk about financial literacy, your view of money, getting on the same page with influencers, and some parameters of progress in creating and accumulating wealth. There are some basics that appear simple but are not easy.

Prudent financial planning and the discipline around it are key tools or instruments. They are like the first violin in the symphony, the conduit, or the fuel that may get you to your destination sooner and better prepared, making it that much more enjoyable when you get there and facilitating a longer stay.

Following are guiding principles, fundamental elements of financial planning, risk elements, and possible rewards brought out by observations and stories. Why are they important to your success and your dreams, and are they possible in your timeframe?

The *why* is your engine. How determined and motivated you are to achieve your vision will generate the money questions, priorities, and steps you need to take? What is your income, earning power, and source now and in the future? What is your spending lifestyle, and what are your future expenses that could affect your net savings or debt levels required to be fiscally fit into the future? Identify the answers to these questions, and do your best to contain risks (i.e., job loss, illness or death, loss of revenue, or property damage). Your tools can range from short-term savings, insurance, access to government programs, and minimizing taxes.

Stay between the guardrails as you grow and age to accumulate wealth, adjust your goals, and react to opportunities. Life events are available, and many, while very important to realizing your dreams, can help steer you there. We financial-analysis geeks are always evaluating the latest trends of new finds and changes in the law and market to factor in. If you aren't one of these geeks, plug into something or someone to be sure you are looking at your finances with a current, customized, and opportunistic lens.

What Does Financial Health Mean to You?

Putting these two words together is somewhat unique to financial planning, but makes more and more sense in my view. A *Forbes* article entitled, "Americans need a fit bit of banking," by Ron Shevlin, seems to further substantiate. This article appeared on June 3, 2019, in communication from Jump Start

Coalition. Jump Start is all about financial education and literacy for young people, which could be an additional resource for you readers.

So what? We haven't been successful cramming financial education down the throats of anyone, as evidenced by surveys on financial education and, just as importantly, preparedness for achieving goals as you grow older.

I believe it is helping people understand *why* this is more important to them or *why* they want to do this, and crafting their vision—then the pieces that are in place.

There seems to be a trend where younger folks are enjoying the present day more, doing things others felt they needed to save their entire lives for; maybe they can have it both ways. If so, good for them!

This *Forbes* article cites three elements to financial health: behavioral, integrated, and measurable. They are defined below:

1. Behavioral: An old concept rooted in literacy and education transformed into a new approach that is behavior driven. It is designed to use technology to help people change financial behaviors and influence decisions.
2. Integrated: Growing research has linked financial health to physical and mental health.
3. Measurable: There is a continuum of financial health, and those components of financial health can be quantified.

This vernacular will come up again. Doesn't it sound like life planning with a spiritual twist and military discipline?

Certifiable Financial Planner

It is important to know the difference between *certified* and *certifiable*. So much of my commentary is firsthand, real-life observations, and much is made of third-party perspectives and insight.

As with anything, there are good planners and not so good (certifiable). Look for credentials, references, and their business model (i.e. fees, commissions, and track record). There are those who make it all about the number you need to be happy; in fact, there's a book entitled *The Number*, by Lee Eisenberg, that expresses this, although he talks about more than the number; he discusses how many focus on just the number, thinking that is all they need to do. Investment performance and consistency versus objectives are all important. The added dimensions of your feelings, and your partner's feelings, about money, goals, dreams (realized and unrealized), passions, and health are equally important. Many things come together for your ultimate happiness and fulfillment.

Depending on the complexity of your resources and objectives, there are degrees of needs, costs, and benefits in working with professionals. Each professional also has a different purpose:

- Investment managers: Help with types of investment vehicles, risk and reward, fees and performance, and track record of performance.

- Attorneys: Help with wills, estates, and managing taxes now and across future generations.
- Insurance Agents: Help to manage risk in your personal and business life.
- Bankers: Help with cash transactions, loans, and deposits.
- Accountants: Help with tax structures and strategies to optimize your tax benefits and net worth contribution.

While this may seem overwhelming, it's manageable and starts with a conversation, some simple tools, steps, and ongoing review, adjusting as circumstances change. While I will talk more about bankers, the process I discuss also applies to identifying and selecting other advisors, building a trusting and mutually beneficial relationship. The advisor you spend more of your time with and give the most trust can very well be the quarterback and help you with identifying others, optimizing the communication and performance of those on your team. Remember, you are still the general manager and your own advocate.

So just a few letters separate certified from certifiable: *ED* for education and *ABLE* to work to quickly disable your plans. Make the right informed choices, and get off the sidelines.

Do Bankers Have Souls?

A friend tells the story that a third of the people she knows don't need a banker, another third don't like their banker, and the other third have reluctantly found a way to work effectively with their banker. A client had requested to sit in on the bank's loan approval committee when his loan was reviewed. This would be insightful, as it might tell you a lot, but it was not likely to occur.

Consider the following when searching for the right banker:

- What is the bank's business model: a large national bank, regional bank, consumer bank, or bank for business?
- What are the bank's history, length of operation, profitability, and agency ratings?
- How and where are decisions being made, and what role, if any, does your assigned banker play in those?
- Who sits on the loan approval committee? Where are they located, and how often do they meet?
- Remember, banking is a highly regulated industry with thin profit margins, and it operates in a risk-averse arena. How was their last regulatory exam?
- Get ahead of communicating when you have challenges, and let the banker know what you plan to do about it. You don't want them to make the call.
- Banks are one of many sources of capital. Understand the options, the costs, and the ground rules.

Most bankers have a soul. It is often locked up tight in the vault with the combination hard to decipher, but when you do, it opens the door to much needed cash and counsel!

What Does the Military Have to Do with Life/Financial Planning?

Certainly, we can see the relevance of discipline to achieving our goals and connect the military to discipline. I am grateful for all those who have served our country with honor, courage, and dedication. While my father served two tours in the military, he never talked about it. He would take my brother and me to war movies, and there were a group of good ones that came out in the '60s, like *Battle of the Bulge* and *Von Ryan's Express*, to name a couple. While I can't go back, and I didn't serve in the military (the Vietnam War was ending, and the draft ended), it also didn't occur to me at the time to explore that route, and my folks had another path in mind for me. My respect and admiration have grown tremendously as my awareness and firsthand experience with the process and the devotion of its people have grown.

I have some very good friends who have served as career soldiers, family members who have served, and good friends who have lost family members to the war.

One of these good friends sent me a *Navy Leader Planning Guide*: excerpts from that on the topic of Principles of Naval Leadership are the following:

- Know yourself, and seek self-improvement.
- Know your family, and look out for their welfare.
- Communicate with your team.
- Make sound and timely decisions.

These are a few battle-tested principles that are critical steps to successful life/financial planning. I saw a number that said about 11 to 12 percent of the population have served in the military, and most of us will not experience the horror and sacrifices of war. We must show our appreciation and respect to them by putting into practice what we have learned from them to contribute in our own way for as long as we are able. We are servants to our families, communities, and country in our own way. Isn't this one of the most rewarding things we can do, at any stage?

Financial Literacy Is Not the Goal

In schools, teachers and coaches struggle with generating interest in conveying the principles and fundamentals of basic financial economic lessons (such as the importance of compound interest, investing early and often, general vocabulary on how to select a financial advisor, managing risk and your psychology and comfort around the whole process).

This is what I mean by financial literacy. As important as it is, it is a tool and a means to an end. Spend time on why this is important to you and your family. What is it you want for your family? Create a formula for health and happiness with:

- a balance between leisure and work
- a type of work where you can grow your legacy
- benchmarks of your progress to avoid bowling with a blindfold on

These goals can be identified and evolving. Your goals are more likely to be achieved if you put in place actions and behaviors stemming from your core beliefs and committing to these goals.

For example, if you want to start a company and you need capital, you can take from your current pay or income stream and automatically deduct it. Then, select an appropriate investment, and apply the principle of compounding, which will get you the amount within a desired timeline. Knowing this and seeing progress will continue to fuel your desire, and the positive reinforcement will strengthen your resolve daily, as you will be tempted by the deluge of ads for things some can't live without.

In a more specific example, a recent headline said that only 16 percent of millennials (ages eighteen to thirty-seven) qualify as financially literate based on a report and survey conducted by Dr. Andrea Hasler, appearing in *Yahoo! Finance*, February 2020, containing three simple questions on numeracy, inflation, and diversification.

1. Suppose you had $100 in a savings account, and the interest rate was 2 percent per year after five years. How much do you think you would have in the account if you left the money to grow? Answers:
   a. more than $102
   b. exactly $102
   c. less than $102

    d. do not know

    e. refuse to answer

2. Imagine that the interest rate on your savings account was 1 percent per year and inflation was 2 percent per year. After one year, how much would you be able to buy with the money in this account? Answers:

    a. more than today

    b. exactly the same

    c. less than today

    d. do not know

    e. refused to answer

3. Please tell me whether this statement is true or false. "Buying a single company stock usually provides a safer return than a stock mutual fund." Answers:

    a. true

    b. false

    c. do not know

    d. refuse to answer

The answers were *a*, *c*, and *b*. Even the millennials who self-identified as financially literate struggled. Only 19 percent of that group was able to answer the three questions correctly.

As I always say, don't tell me I need to know the time value of money; help me identify, map out, and begin the journey to my summit, and how the time value of money will help me get there. I *might* be listening then.

A San Diego-based financial literacy platform called iGrad was recently founded by President Rob La Breche.

iGrad has launched the first financial wellness assessment to teach the why behind financial decision making and recommended personality-based positive changes. Developed by leading financial wellness behavior experts "Your Money Personality"TM helps people gain insight into how the personality influences everything from budgeting to saving for retirement and then teaches us how to make better financial decisions. More than 600 universities use the iGrad financial wellness platform.

Financial Planning Standards

These are ground rules, regulations, and standards around genuine financial planning. Whether you're using an advisor or doing it yourself, please know what the standards are.

1. Understanding the client's personal and financial circumstances
2. Identifying and selecting your goal
3. Analyzing the client's current course of action and potential alternative courses of action
4. Developing the financial planning recommendations
5. Presenting the financial planning recommendations
6. Implementing the financial planning recommendations
7. Monitoring progress in updating your financial plan

The point here is that you can tackle this on your own. You can do part of it in phases or hire a professional who is proven, experienced, and recommended. Either way, write it down, refer to it, talk about it, make adjustments, and repeat. If you don't write it down, don't waste your time—go back to dreamland, and don't wake up, because for many, it may seem like a nightmare if you're not prepared. I highly recommend dreaming with a dose of documentation.

Psychology of Financial Planning

Financial planning is becoming more automated through robo- (automated) investing and planning and self-administration through access to tools many firms offer the consumer to lower expenses. They engage early adopters and attract the emerging wealthy. As a result, more and more niche emphasis is on the value of human interaction, advice, and support. This further substantiates the holistic approach to life's journey and how financial resources are inextricably linked.

One discipline emerging, and promoted on the website of the Center for Financial Planning, is a program for advisors in clinical psychology offered at the Wharton University of Pennsylvania. A few of the learning objectives are as follows:

- Become more client centered.
- Better knowledge of client psychology and decision-making can help you build deeper, long-lasting customer relationships.
- Help clients achieve better outcomes.
- Understand how clients' psychology can guide clients toward better decisions.

- Develop new insights into a surge of millennial clients with different views of financial planning.
- An element of clinical psychology includes spending, savings, and money disorders.

Client psychology is a growing field that merges traditional financial knowledge with an understanding of the best practices from aspects of finance, financial planning, and the variety of the human sciences.

In a podcast from the knowledge at Wharton featuring Kevin Keller, Charles Chaffin, and Christopher Geczy, they talk about a transition from transactional to holistic in the financial planning space, moving from product to process and establishing a customer lifetime value, rising against individual financial solutions and transactions.

Very often, you will see the industry focus their resources toward those with greater than $500,000 of investable assets, leaving those with less than that to fend for themselves. This is where technology and robo-investing may be a partial solution. Regardless of the dollars you have to invest, there is the holistic process, self-awareness, personality, and risk profile: your goals are up to you.

Like it or not, our medical profession and health sciences are moving in the same direction. It's hard to find a general practitioner who feels they can devote the time with the patient, continue to build medical acumen, pay off student loans, pay for malpractice insurance, and still have a rewarding career and profession. You may be seen by a remote doctor through video, or taken care of by a relatively new practitioner, nurse, or physician's assistant, or perhaps the pharmacist.

If you've known someone in the hospital for more serious issues, they likely have had a group of specialists deep in the knowledge of the area of expertise. You have heard some say the patient or the family needs to be their own advocate. The patient/family may be the only one who has a grasp of what each specialist is proposing, but not really, as the patient isn't typically a medical professional.

I make this point, as you need to be your own advocate in the life and financial planning area. I have cited the CFP standards and process elsewhere in this book. Just as you probably check your own vitals pulse, blood pressure, and temperature before going to the doctor, you need to take your own vitals in your financial area:

- Statement of assets and liabilities
- Statement of income and expenses
- Your net outflow/inflow (i.e., cash flow)
- Documentation of your short-term and long-term goals
- Bank and investment statements, fees paid, and net investment returns over time
- Annual financial physical

You got this! Get started, talk about it, seek professional advice, and you'll be amazed at how healthy and strong the patient grows to be.

Replace the Green Carpet

Talking about our relationship with money, and how it can and should be the means to a more fulfilling life, makes a lot of sense intellectually. What muddles that up is the hecticness of life—what comes at us, and just as important, how we grew up and the role money played in at all.

My wife and I were newly married and starting a family, and we had no, or very little, savings. I grew up feeling like we had everything we needed; I saw my mom working hard at home with five kids and dad working hard at his job. Back then, one worked hard, lived modestly but comfortably, and tried to think about saving for the future: maybe college, retirement, or a second car. I don't know what is normal; in fact, there is no normal.

Well, when we bought our first house, it was a little bit of a stretch, and a new commitment. I probably said something like, "We can't spend any money for three years because of our new mortgage." Well, that lasted a few months, and this nice older home had some outdated, worn out, and ugly green carpet in the main room.

We tried to budget, as my wife and I were on one income with one child at home, and tried not to let emotion enter in. Well, that didn't work so well. The green carpet became a symbol for the devil or an albatross or all that was wrong in the world.

We went back and forth for a year or two, trying to put a little in the college fund and just get started on a small retirement savings. While I went somewhere else to work every day,

Katy was at home working and raising our daughters—and staring at the green carpet.

Yes, we eventually replaced it with a nice beige, probably about the time we were moving to a bigger house.

As it turned out, Katy and I were forming our combined views as a young family on money, priorities, needs, and wants, and we could have had a little better understanding and discipline around what we were making and spending and why.

You know, decades later, with large expenditures, Katy always reminds me it is the green carpet all over again. So save some time and headaches, give money and priorities a little thought and discussion, and just replace the green carpet!

SUMMARY AND ACTIVITY

Summary

- Most bankers have a soul; it is just often locked up tight in the vault. Find a way to build a relationship with your banker.
- Financial literacy is not the end goal; rather, it is a means to an end.
- Write down your financial goals and plans down, and continue to expand on them.
- Address your own form of the ugly green carpet.

Activity

Document in detail a statement of your assets and liabilities, and date this entry in order to see your growth. Date_____

Write down your major annual expenses and sources and amounts of net income, forming some sort of organized budget.

Seek competent counsel, within your means, and use the prior notes of this section to put a documented financial plan in place.

Take Some Risks

*Many view God as an airman views a parachute, it's
there for emergencies, but they hope to never need it.*
—C. S. Lewis

We don't tend to think about the risk-reward continuum too
often in all of life's day-to-day decisions: it is instinct, faith,
routine, experience growing up, and losing and winning. For
example, think about driving and the myriad of subconscious
decisions to follow the rules, stay in your lane, anticipate other
drivers, engage oncoming drivers, implement timing and reflex-
es, even while tailgating or being tailgated when in a hurry. You
wouldn't leave the house if you thought about all these things all
the time. Of all the considerations in doing the right thing, there
are two in particular that I think are worthwhile noting in this.

Spirituality: A faith and trusting when you're not sure. This
is a force that mitigates risk, even though you can't see it or truly know it's here. Faith in human nature/spirit, and the greater

good, can guide you to do the right thing, and preserve life and safety. Scientists would tell you more, but they can't explain it all. Human nature is at work reactively, whether we choose it or not. It can work for us consciously and proactively. Spirituality can reassure and empower you to know no boundaries. You can invest in it, be aware of it, depend on it, and nurture it, and then great gifts result for many who do, like peace, comfort, hope, and inspiration.

How Much Can You Bench Press?

If you've exercised at a fitness facility, perhaps you have found yourself stepping into a piece of equipment that had a certain amount of weight on it, say fifty pounds. As you are trying to lift it, or push it, or move it in the direction called for, you just can't quite do it.

This can be terrifying, especially if you follow someone, and they have lifted fifty pounds, and you know you can only do twenty-five. For me, that is a blow to my psyche that I can't lift as much as the prior person, whom I didn't even see. Now, if I can lift seventy-five pounds rather than the fifty pounds hoisted by the person before, then I am feeling pretty good about myself.

I know this sounds a little crazy, but how often do we compare ourselves to others with no idea of their circumstances? As I look around the gym, there are people from their twenties and thirties, and all the way to their eighties. How often do we think we know about the other person by how much they can bench press, or worse, how much we can lift compared to them?

As I have spent some time working in banks, you have to make decisions about people, especially if you plan on lending them some of the bank's money. Let me just say that what people provide the bank in the way of a financial statement, and how it appears or how they say they live their lives, doesn't always add up.

I say this because I probably wasted a lot of time giving any thought to what someone might think about what I do, and what I say, when the truth is they are more concerned with their own lives than mine. Putting myself out there with this book is perhaps a step in the right direction!

So what I try to do now is to acknowledge I know very little about most people I come into contact with, or what I think is wrong. I am now more aware of really trying to get to know their story, even a little bit about them from their own voice.

A new friend of mine commented (as we shared a cup of coffee, in response to my saying they didn't have internet service at a new coffee shop) that yes, it was very interesting to observe everyone's behavior when they realized their technology didn't work, and they actually had to interact with one another.

It was refreshing to hear that perspective. So walk up to someone and say, "Please tell me your story." We might all learn something.

Military Discipline

The other thing in managing life's risks where I find an example to emulate is military discipline. The military prepares for the biggest risk of losing your life, giving your life, and protecting others' lives (for that matter, so does spirituality). The discipline in our daily habits, precision in decisions and carrying them out, cause us to be better prepared for our days and our lives and learn to anticipate and respond well to situations. We will talk more about military honor, and recognize the institution, trying to offer a couple of personal examples that we can apply to the world of financial and life planning.

According to one definition, military discipline is created within a command by instilling a sense of confidence and responsibility in each individual. It helps build character and contributes to a cohesive team. As cited in the Citizen Soldier Resource Center on Military Discipline, by Chuck Holmes, "Discipline is the major difference between a bad soldier and an excellent soldier." It's the basic foundation of any successful military unit or officer: holding yourself and others to a higher standard.

Following are examples of military discipline that I believe apply to success in life planning:

- Respect others.
- Place the good of the unit above others.
- Always give 100 percent.
- Do what you say you will do.
- Take pride in everything that you do.
- Be accountable for your actions in your followers' actions.
- Obey policies and regulations.
- Maintain physical fitness.
- Maintain proficiencies.
- Do the right thing.

Consider the risk-reward continuum, referred to Senator Tom Cotton's book titled *Sacred Duty*; he was a member of the Old Guard in 2007 and 2008. The Old Guard was instituted in 1784 and welcomes fallen soldiers home to Dover Air Force Base in Washington, DC and presides over the Tomb of the Unknown Soldier and over many formal ceremonies in Washington, DC, at the White House and Capitol. I use this as an example of discipline and precision and why it is that way.

Senator Cotton states in his book, "Once we entered Arlington national cemetery our standard was nothing short of perfection. The Old Guard can conduct more than 20 funerals per day. But, for the fallen and their families each funeral is unique to a once-in-a-lifetime moment. As Old Guard soldiers, we viewed the funerals through their eyes as we trained, prepared our uniforms and performed the rituals of Arlington. We held ourselves to the standard of perfection. Every funeral is a no fail, zero-defect mission."

Whatever your mission, journey to your summit, or making the most of each day, properly focused discipline will contribute to your success. Even the little things and steps can have a significant impact and will likely mean a lot to those in your life.

We tend to think about the big risks in life with the rewards that come with it, what we can gain, what we can lose, and the impact on those around us. Maybe a T-chart or a spreadsheet to help us. Are you performing with a net, or are you potentially making a fatal mistake? We tend to try to bowl with bumper guards, always staying on course and not going in the gutter.

Risks in life, such as investing, can't be avoided. If you learn to think about them and manage them, you may be pleasantly surprised, have fewer regrets, and accomplish beyond what you thought was possible.

What Is Your Deepest Fear?

I recall a successful client who was talking about selling his business for $15 million. He had built it from nothing over twenty-five years. The words *relieved, relaxed, happy-go-lucky,* and *excited* were not in his vernacular—he was scared out of his mind. This happened suddenly; he was so into the elements of running his business and pulling all those levers, and then it was converted to a pile of money. His comfort zone disappeared. While it wasn't easy, it became what he knew, framing his everyday decision-making as the object of his daily routine and energy. He was afraid of making the wrong decision about his money, losing it all, having to start over, and comprehending what he didn't know about his new world.

If you are a sports movie buff, perhaps you've seen the movie called *Coach Carter*. Coach Carter coaches to success a group of disadvantaged young men, ill-equipped to deal with life, much less basketball. Coach Carter asked one of the young men a riddle in the form of a question: "What is your deepest fear, young man?" After much time and thought and dramatic lessons learned, the young men answered,

"Our deepest fear is not that we are inadequate. Our deepest fear is that we are powerful beyond measure.

It is our light, not our darkness that most frightens us. Your playing small does not serve the world. There is nothing enlightening about shrinking so that other people won't feel insecure around you. We are all meant to shine as children do. It's not just in some of us, it's in everyone. And as we let our own lights shine, we unconsciously give other people permission to do the same. As we are liberated from our own fear, our presence automatically liberates others."

This quote is attributed to Marianne Williamson (incorrectly now and then to Nelson Mandela) from a book she wrote in 1992. I liked this when I first heard it and believe it to be a good framework for tackling your fears, challenging yourself, and journeying to your summit. If you have connected the dots, I don't believe it helped her win the nomination for presidency in 2020, but perhaps it might be cause for further consideration.

Lead from Any Position

Do you know people who take charge, know themselves, know where they want to go, act with courage, and naturally inspire? Yes? Did they have the biggest title and position? Very often not. They may have been an entry-level role, customer service, sales associate, or an intern. Maybe they are born that way, but likely not. Along the way, they developed curiosity and found determination, a work ethic, some confidence, and a willingness to acknowledge defeat, learn, and persevere.

In the movie *Four Christmases*, Vince Vaughn and Reese Witherspoon get drafted into the Christmas nativity play. He gets into his role as Joseph, Jesus's father, and gets a bit carried away, but people loved it. He embraced the responsibility and his chance to influence. This reminds me of someone once telling me that in every class or seminar they attend, they sit in the front row. If you are going to attend, be all in.

I was tested, as I mentioned, when my wife, Katy, and I volunteered at Vacation Bible School for a group of kids, including four of our grandkids. I was the assistant volunteer. My ego was OK, so I tried being the best dang assistant volunteer—as if I had the role of Joseph or Santa Claus. These little kids won't care about my title or background, but they will know if I like being there and know what I am doing, as I am enthusiastic and capturing their attention. If you can keep the attention and interest of a three-to-five-year-old audience, the rest is easy!

Run, Forrest, Run

We all make decisions, often with little time and a big dose of innate or developed judgment. There's a whole subject on behavioral finance and natural biases for another time.

I have had my share of good and not-so-good decisions. I have learned how much I don't know and how snap judgments can be way off.

With a little creative license, there are some great lessons taken from the movie *Forrest Gump*. If you saw that movie, he was portrayed as simple—he didn't let anyone tell him what to think or what he couldn't do. He didn't seem to have a plan; he just started running, playing Ping-Pong and football, and shrimping with more success than anyone thought possible.

Forrest got out and took some risks with a core value system and work ethic, and it worked. He found himself with some amazing people, in very compelling surroundings, and was fortunate and grateful. Successful people didn't always have this grand strategy; they see opportunity and were not afraid to act on their strong drive and moral compass.

It seems to me that Forrest Gump was pretty smart after all. Unlike those who are tentative and not sure where they are going, but making good time, the "Forrest Gump effect" can be a pretty good lesson.

Run, Forrest, run.

Did You Know That as You Age, so Does Your Cursing?

I have been warned about four-letter words since I was too young to remember. For some strange reason, I recall being very young, maybe five or six, jumping around in the back seat of our family station wagon before there were seat belts. Mom and Dad were in the front seat, driving on the Milwaukee freeway, where the skyline was dotted with huge beer signs. Trying to impress with my early reading skills, when we passed a big Schlitz beer sign, I took a stab at sounding it out. While my parents were trying hard not to laugh, they told me what I said was inappropriate. You can guess my five-year-old mind's derivation of Schlitz beer.

So, it began…growing and aging through a number of phases. The following is age appropriate; now the swearing I do or hear involves some of the following words:

- "I used to…"
- "…for your age"
- "Act your age!"
- "Happy birthday!"

Think about how many times you say or think, "I used to do that." Some of that may be because of changing interests, perhaps some legitimate constraints, but often it is attitude or societal limitations.

You do that pretty well for a person of your age. Check out the book *Younger Next Year*, by Crowley and Lodge. It is a series on getting healthier as you age and more able in many ways. A good friend, at age sixty-four, just biked 4,500 miles in fifty-three days and is planning his next 3,000-mile trek. Clearly, he trains, and one needs to use common sense, but be aware we are limited by our own thinking and opinions of others, and… remember what your parents told you about cursing!

Curiosity Cured the Cat

Or is that *killed* the cat? If you are reading this, either way, you are likely curious, a continual learner, looking to do things better, faster, stronger and make a difference.

After returning from hiking in the Smoky Mountains with dear friends, and hiking the Appalachian Trail, a few profound thoughts (or what appeared to be profound thoughts at the time) popped up. There was much time to think and get others' perspectives as you speculate on the hundreds of folks in the park on a Wednesday in October. When I was working full time, I thought no one would be in a national park on a Wednesday, but again, I digress.

The husband of our friends just retired, and he was talking about the experience—his view, what he thought was his wife's view of it, and so forth. While she was listening and reacting, she commented that she had her "Aha!" moment in big transition when the kids left the house. She got used to her situation, put some goals and discipline around it, and got her rhythm. She talked about how difficult it was to watch the sausage being made (an old Wisconsin saying), which her husband was not around for when she went through it.

How many times is your curiosity killed, along with the cat, or nurtured to learn a perspective, put yourself out there, and apply new ideas? I think about this in a crowded elevator, on a train or plane ride, while waiting in a queue, or when seeing someone with a Green Bay packer jersey in South Carolina. Do you take that risk? And put forth the effort? I know I often don't. Look how much I am missing out on learning something new.

In fact, the accomplished author Malcom Gladwell has written a new book called *Talking to Strangers*. In it, he talks about people's tendencies to make lots of assumptions (often wrong ones) about people, resulting in erroneous paths.

As a social introvert, I am trying to feed my curiosity in a number of ways. What's the risk? I do have eight more lives.

Eighty-Six and No Regrets

We were very fortunate; my siblings and I had our mom with us for a long time, having lost our dad at a much younger age. Her health had taken a turn, and we felt we needed to talk about some things. She was sharp as a tack, and my brother and sisters and I had a lot of fun with her. I can tell you, I wish I had asked more questions about her life and my dad's, and paid more attention to the answers.

She was the youngest of eight in a large Irish-Catholic family. As the youngest of eight, she said there were squabbles— good times and tough times. She had a happy and healthy marriage and family with my dad, and it sure seemed like a pretty full life. Being the oldest, I am sure I challenged her certainly in my teen years, and while we are a close family, she was the mother, and we were the kids, and that was all good with us.

In one of our conversations the last year of her life, I asked her if she had any regrets about things she might have done differently. When I was much younger, she would say my listening skills were sometimes lacking growing up; she would more directly say, "Get the wax out of your ears, and don't make me tell you again to clean up your room!" My point is that I was listening intently to her answer to my genuine question about regrets.

She thought about it a bit, and very thoughtfully, she said, "I suppose if I really had wanted to do something different, I would have done it."

My first reaction was that it might be a standard response or a dodge to the question. But the way she said it, and the more I thought about it, the more profound it sounded.

Life is a series of choices; assuming we have free will, we evaluate and make decisions and act accordingly, but we have choices. We are blessed and fortunate to have them and to be able to make the call. They don't always work out, so you go back to square one, but life turned out for my mom the way she had in mind. She didn't choose to lose my dad in their fifties, and it was devastating, but we all pulled together and did our best to get on with life.

It probably does not make a lot of sense to look back, regret, and rethink past decisions, because you lose precious current moments. If you truly want to do something different, with all your heart and soul, then really consider going out and doing it. If you choose not to, then check your reasoning—make the call, and don't look back. Thanks, Mom; I am still listening and learning.

Navy Life Experiences

I wanted to capture a small real life sample of how the navy prepares people, and how it can positively contribute to your life planning either through firsthand experience or observations of others. My contention is that military principles and discipline are of value to those seeking life and financial success. My dear friend, retired commander Rob Goodwin, willfully contributed his advice and stories to this book, to share from his perspective.

Focus on Your Life

As a young naval officer, I was standing on the fantail of the USS *Moosebrucker*, talking to my officer-in-charge. When I walked up, he was staring off into the sky.

I asked him what he was thinking about. He said, "You know, I make more money than the captain of this ship [he received flight pay], but that's not what is important. What is important is that I don't make any less."

This attitude exemplifies the attitude of most military people. The pay rate is published, so everyone knows what everyone else makes. You don't work for bonuses or higher annual increases; you work for what you want. If you want to make more money, then you gravitate toward a specialty that increases your pay, or you become one of the "best" military people in your organization, which causes you to advance in rank more quickly.

This attitude is the realization that money isn't important and that no amount of money will garner everything you want. The important thing is to balance what you want out of life with the desired lifestyle. Having more than enough money probably means you are missing out on parts of life that will be important later on, like family.

P.S.: Having enough money also means you are saving for retirement.

Ethics

The military has a phrase that goes something like this: "I will do nothing or give the appearance thereof..." This phrase has been with me for most of my life and has been taken to heart.

You see, in the military, you are likely to get in a dangerous situation at some point in your career. When this happens, your very life may be in the hands of the person standing next to you or manning one of the battle stations. How would you like knowing that the person on whom you depended was a liar or someone prone to making bad decisions?

The person I want standing on either side of me is someone who has a good moral foundation with a practiced record of making good decisions for himself and those around him. I never want to doubt that we are in the situation together, and together we will figure it out.

In seems like today's society has forgotten this simple truth and works hard to stretch the truth or believe that its everyone else's job to do the right thing. In a dicey situation, you are more likely to be thrown under the bus, as opposed to coming together shoulder-to-shoulder to work through the issue.

I miss my military friends who watched my back twenty-four seven!

Military Life

Often in the newspapers, magazines, and TV, news you will hear about the tough lives of military families. The focus is on the moves that take place about every three years, military housing, perhaps the low pay, or arduous work conditions. While all these statements are true, I was a military person with a military family, and the focus is all wrong.

I am going to skip recounting my path through the military as a single officer, then a young navy pilot, and then as naval officer with a family. The important part of each stage was the similarity in the naval family. You see, each family pretty much traveled the same route.

Every person in your military specialty experienced the same things. They made the same amount of money. They lived in the same sort of housing. They all wrestled with the moving, deploying, and making new friends. The reason this wasn't a challenge is that the more experienced folks took a personal pleasure in showing the less experienced families the ropes. There was no "gain" for the time and trouble for helping the "newbies," and there was none expected. It is the way of life where you love your neighbors as yourself, knowing that one day you will need the same sort of coaching.

I am now out of the military and have lived in many civilian neighborhoods. Often, neighbors never see each other and consequently don't know one another. Kids no longer have pickup games. The new model is to get your kid enrolled in a travel league, which further diminishes the neighborhood unit. This is a sad commentary on life in America today.

Now, I am retired. Recently, a pilot who went through flight school with me forty years ago and I were reacquainted. I can't tell you how much we enjoyed talking about the old days when we were single and then bragging about our wives and kids. The wife of another gentleman (we lived in the same military housing while going through naval postgraduate school together) was there for my wife when she was nervous about having our first child. He was there to watch the dog when my first child was born. In between, they had us over for dinner (a lost art), shared their family with us (we really enjoyed their two daughters and their son), and in a way, we grew up together.

The thought I'd like to leave you with is that military life is often hard, but then, so is life in general. I wouldn't trade my military years for anything. I didn't like being away from home and family, but the extended military family was always there to help me over the rough spots. Now, in retirement, I am finding that they are still around, still care about our friendship, and are still wonderful people!

SUMMARY AND ACTIVITY

Summary
- Successful people don't always have a grand strategy; they see opportunity and want to act on their strong drive and their moral compass.
- Faith and spirituality can provide comfort, confidence, and clarity in a seemingly chaotic time.
- Military discipline prepares for the biggest risk of saving lives. We can learn from that.
- You can't eliminate risk. Be aware of it, manage it, and capitalize on it.

Activity
What is your deepest fear about your future?

What can you do to manage what is standing in your way of accomplishing your dreams?

What is something you currently regret in terms of your finances? What did you learn from this situation, and how can you do better?

Balance and Perspective

Isn't it funny how day-to-day nothing changes, but
when you look back, everything is different?
—C. S. Lewis

Perspective through Passionate Curiosity

An amazing, prolific author stated her success was due to always pursuing her passionate curiosity. She would go where no
one typically would go, in pursuit of subjects like snakes and
spiders and relevant social issues, often in children's books. Her
name is Kate Messner. We all have the ability to venture out of
our lane, now and then, and discover a tributary and pursue it.
Often it leads nowhere, but sometimes it pays off.

She also had some insight when asked at a conference
about where she and others get their ideas for their next book.
She said she used to think that the idea would come to her
while she was waiting to be inspired. Of course, there were
many days of waiting with nothing materializing. Then she

learned that the most successful and prolific authors read and wrote continuously. They did not wait; they went after it. They chased and sought out inspiration where others didn't or failed to follow through. She didn't know where it would end or if it would pay off, but she was determined to make her own path and not wait for the apple to fall on her head.

I've heard many say to me that they are not sure what their passion is and are waiting to figure it out. Well, here is an example; you need to seek it and pursue a number of things to find it, as waiting for it may never become clear.

James Patterson has sold nearly four hundred million books across a myriad of genres, from suspense thrillers to young adult books. He has reinvented writing through his style and depth, and his productivity turned the publishing industry on its ear. He will often write an eighty-page outline, and someone will come in and finish it, as he is off to the next book. These are examples cited in the *Washington Post* article on Mr. Patterson June 6, 2016. He is a publishing factory and an amazingly generous philanthropist, funding hundreds of teachers' salaries, libraries, and individual bookstores. This is all particularly impressive, when I learned his first book was rejected thirty-one times!

The point of all this is to read, write, act, and relate relentlessly, and you will craft your own path, purpose, and plan, reaching your summit and optimizing your resources and talents along the way. It is not something that stops or starts at a certain age or time—and how fulfilling is that to know you will make the most of your time at any age?

There is much to be done here, just as you would tune up your car or instead risk a breakdown—not necessarily a right or wrong way, just being aware, determining your happy place, and adjusting.

Anything you can do to step outside of yourself and the situation, to better see it and appreciate other's positions, is important. This empathy is invaluable in optimizing your pathway and gathering support, and leaving a positive impact, or the opposite will occur: leaving a wake of destruction and negativity. I like disruption, not destruction. Disruption challenges, changes it up, encourages new ideas, and results often in breakthroughs of happiness and fulfillment.

Professionally, you can achieve this if you have done other people's jobs along the way. Talk with a mentor, or be a mentee to understand other jobs, leaders, industries, and competitors. A big way to do this is ongoing education, such as courses in your field on leadership, industry designations, and self-study.

Life and Leadership

Some see the destination and find a way to it. Some don't see the destination but are determined and effective at making the most of every day. Is leadership innate or learned, and why is it relevant to a fulfilling life? Why invest time in learning about it, and what do you have to show for it?

Having participated in many sessions on leadership, attended week-long seminars, read countless books on the topic, and even been asked to talk about it at classes and seminars, I have observed many good and not-so-good leaders.

I believe leadership is both innate and learned. It is a lot about bringing to the conscious level, preparing for the unexpected, and exploring scenarios you would want to do under various circumstances.

Good leaders have core beliefs and values, morals, and convictions; knowing them, sharing them, and practicing them can make you a better person and those around you better people. It can be subtle, if untested in a big way, yet still effective.

I attended a two-week program at the University of Virginia Darden School of Business on leadership. Thirty of us came together, partly because it was part of our job development in a larger regional bank. I am not patient at doing something I don't want to do or feel as if I don't have a choice in, but this is a long time to be immersed in the subject, and we heard from some of the best.

I wasn't exactly sure how, but I found myself leading a dancing chain of twenty-five people singing Manfred Mann's "Do Wah Diddy Diddy" and organizing a 5:00 a.m. hot air balloon ride over Charlottesville, Virginia. Maybe I wanted to make the time pass, or maybe I felt a bit inspired to make a memory with my peers.

It's prepping for the tests and circumstances life throws your way. Leadership, courage, and motivation of others are tested every day from those who are working in the military, to first responders, or to truly extending yourself. For most of us, it is really not tested too often. But the qualities, zeroing in on why you are living your life and finding your larger purpose, help navigate everyday events and decisions.

If you don't know your grand plan, no worries; learning about leadership helps you make simple day-to-day decisions that I assume will get you to a grand plan, perhaps not one that is readily visible, but that nonetheless is real and rewarding. Learning about leadership gets you off the couch and in the game. It is not a spectator sport.

So pick up a book on leadership, study it, and talk to good leaders you know. Continue to bring out the best in you and those around you. It will add to your enjoyment in life every day, and most certainly, when you are looking at your life in the rearview mirror.

I'm so humbled by some good friends I am fortunate to know who have reached the highest military ranks, fought fiercely in battle, seen the worst that war and tragedy bring our way, and dedicated their lives to service. They are role models to me, but they would deny they are heroes. They would tell you they are just like you and me. My point is that today and tomorrow, on whatever stage you call life, why wait for someone else to step up? Prepare yourself, and take the plunge; you'll be glad you did for all the right reasons.

The Four-Legged Stool

With balance, I can tell you my four-legged stool (yours may have three or five legs) has always been a little wobbly. Sometimes I put rolled-up cardboard under a leg to fix it temporarily; sometimes I actually put a more permanent fix in place. My four legs are intellectual, physical, social, and spiritual outcomes. Many of my stories or vignettes further these areas. You have to design your stool, what amount of time is right for you, and where you are at, or when you are in your ideal balance.

Some would say successful people don't have balance; in *The Outlier Effect*, Malcolm Gladwell talks of investing ten thousand hours in something to be effective. That may not leave much time for anything else; examples are Microsoft's Bill Gates, NFL Green Bay Packers coach Vince Lombardi, pro golfer Tiger Woods, and Apple CEO Steve Jobs.

Generally, for most of us, investing in your health with physical activity with nutrition, and adjusting it along the way, yet being consistent, is important. Have the habits that sustain; avoid starting and stopping, but get started. Frankly, for me, exercise has been my prescription to help with my hyperactivity, competitiveness, ego, and frugality (I do not want to spend money on new clothes). As a self-defined control freak, to some degree, this is something I can impact, although I regularly get distracted and go off the regimen now and then.

Intellectual

The intellectual part of your stool is the myriad of ways to work your brain. Active brain health gets more attention these days. Use it or lose it—in every sense of the phrase. Get immersed in something that gets your mind off the mundane and routines, that teaches you something and challenges you to work and use all parts of your mind.

I probably shook some important things loose in nearly twelve years of playing tackle football, so I don't necessarily recommend that, but I wouldn't change it, and I will blame the deficiencies in this material on a concussion or two.

Social

The social part varies based on your extroversion or introversion tendencies, but either way, be aware of it, and bring people into your life when and how you can. You need it, as you receive energy from the right mix of people.

True friendship is one of life's rewards and contributes to one's longevity and happiness. Friends are rare and to be cherished. We have moved around a bit, and it's interesting that there are many categories of friends. Everyone has or has had one—friends who are your best pal, engaged, friendly, and have things in common. It is great while it lasts, but something changes with them. They may be very good people, but you move, or they move, down the block, dropping off the face of the earth; there is no response, no effort, nothing. You realize they are a friend of convenience (FOC); you were convenient, helped them, were accessible, and made life comfortable and reassuring for them. But now, there is no time for old friends, and they have moved on to bigger and better things: you have been FOC'd. Maybe I am a little cynical and unfair, and perhaps I, too, have been a friend of convenience, but think about it—true friends will be there for you and invest time in your relationship through thick and thin. They will definitely be in the asset column, the plus column. Find one, keep one, and cherish that person always.

Hey, Are You Someone?

Normally, I am rushing around with ten things on my mind, in my own little world, and not thinking about those around me or even why I might be running around like a nut. I've done this much of my life, and many of us do the same thing. We are missing so many opportunities to get more out of the lives we live if we take but a moment.

One of my pastimes is periodically taking a class outside of my degree and profession to offer perspective and use another part of the brain I have left. I was walking through the massive library of the university I was attending as a nontraditional student (not sure I ever was a truly traditional student). I saw a middle-aged woman working very hard at wet-mopping the hardwood floors as people were walking around her and through her work. I walked past her so as to not trample her work but to be in earshot, and I said to her, "The floors look great. Thank you for your hard work and terrific job!"

She looked up, a bit stunned, and then she smiled and said, "Who are you? I mean, are you someone at the top?" She held her hand above her head, meaning some top brass at the university. I smiled more broadly and said, "No, no, I'm nobody." As I kept walking, I could hear her say, "No, sir, yes, sir, you certainly are somebody!" A fun exchange maybe we both will be talking about for a while.

Take a moment to realize that we all are somebody, and we can contribute to someone's well-being, even if we are not at the top of the food chain. Being aware of others' situations can help balance your social stool leg.

Spirituality

Spiritually, we can see the wonderful benefits of things we can't see but are in our lives. Accept it, explore it, nurture it, and believe what you will, but embrace this intangible force in your way. There is much we don't know and can't explain that influences our lives; it is at work and nudges us. You may not attribute it to God, your religion, or anything tangible. I refer to this as spirituality and believe there to be a force by which we are guided. Rather than thinking of this as my attempt at conversion, it can be seen that spirituality in general can offer an element of life's satisfaction that, when acknowledged and nurtured, would likely add much to your journey.

From Monk to Money Manager is an actual nonfiction book penned by Doug Lynam. It is about planning with a spiritual twist, understanding your relationship with money and outcomes. It discusses approaching life and financial planning in a holistic, healthy, deep, and penetrating way together to align your resources with your faith, hope, and charity. Doug Lynam was a monk for many years, eschewing the wealth of his family. He was asked to do the books and financial records of the monastery, and he connected the dots between a satisfying life and financial literacy over years, moving onto a financial career.

While money is hard and real, and numbers are what they are and don't lie, what they tell you and what you do with the information to leverage your dreams and contribute to others' well-being gives the spiritualistic opportunity and the trust and faith that there is much more to be done.

There are lots of examples over the centuries of the abuse of money and power in almost every church and religion, often resulting in new beliefs and religions (the Lutheran church as an example). If it can be misused, why can't the opposite be true? Money and planning can be used for leveraging good, bringing people together, and achieving many positive hopes and dreams.

Bishop Fulton Sheen hosted radio and television shows, one entitled *Life is Worth Living*. It was an award-winning show, which spent nearly thirty years on the air. In fact, Bishop Sheen is well on the way to becoming the first male American-born saint. His niece, Joan Sheen Cunningham, spent time with him while she schooled in New York and tells the story that she and her uncle would often be approached as they walked the sidewalks of New York and asked for money by those in need. Bishop Sheen would pull out a twenty-dollar bill and hand it to them. She asked him how he knew they were really in need, and he said, "I can't take that chance."

Can you take the chance that your life and financial plans can't be used for your good and the well-being of those around you? That seems to me to be doing the work of spirituality, and a risk not worth taking.

One Step Closer to God
I was talking to my granddaughter about driving a car, taking her sister for a ride, and all the independence that comes with that—she's five. She said, "Papa, that's nice, but what do you know? And you may not be around then because you're old." And she's right!

While I am still pretty spry and as immature as the next guy, it got me thinking that each day, each of us is one step closer to God. I happen to believe that. Whatever you believe, it is still a reminder of finite time on Planet Earth.

So this should be a theme or idea woven into the fabric of your retirement plan—not to be morbid or depressing, but to accept, prepare, and make the most of every day here we have here. Don't ignore it or live in that great state of denial! In fact, many people aren't given this opportunity and would love to be in your shoes but were cheated out of it.

In your life planning (while sounding counterintuitive), embrace your mortality, your faith and spirituality, and that of others in your life, and rejoice in knowing you are one step closer to God!

I asked dear friends Jean and Joe about their personal experience . Their response follows:

"How does spirituality contribute to your success in life?" For starters, can we change the question to be about faith instead of spirituality? It might seem like mincing words a bit, but Jean and I almost never talk about spirituality. However, we talk about faith quite a bit. We talk about "living our faith", not "living our spirituality". Spirituality, I think, is broader, more philosophical, and asks the question "what is the meaning of life?" For us, faith provides the answer to that question, and as such it is more tangible, more actionable. So, with that preamble – here's our answer to the question: "how does faith contribute to your success in life?"

When we're living life as best we can, our faith in God is the thing that drives everything else. Mother Teresa summed it up best, "God does not require that we be successful, only that we be faithful." Knowing that God created us, that He loves us, and that He has certain expectations for us is the basis by which our decisions are made and consequently by which "success" is defined. Success is the alignment of our actions with what He wants for us. We've found (and seen in others) that this approach is the path to peace and joy - regardless of life's circumstances. When we let our faith lead us, we make different decisions than if we let our own desires or the pressures/trends of society drive us. Faith drives every aspect of our lives – financial, relationships, our marriage, our parenting, careers, etc. When we follow God's lead (as we've done with Jean's volunteering, my career change, Jean's cancer episodes, our decision to become Big Brother and Big Sister to Jamel, and so many others), life becomes richer, more interesting, and more satisfying. Of course, we fall short many times – but our faith is the thing that always draws us back to the path that we know is right for us. In that regard, St. Augustine had it right, "You have made us for yourself, O Lord, and our heart is restless until it rests in you."

It's a Small World, after All

I recently visited Disney World with our kids and grand-kids after a twenty-five-year hiatus from when our kids were small. It was very fun to see Disney again through the eyes and expressions of small children: our five grandkids under the age of six. While a lot had changed, one ride/attraction did not seem to be different: "It's a Small, Small World." If you have experienced this, you know it's about seeing the world through the eyes of children and how much we have in common with our customs and cultures of many other countries—how important it is to live in peace and harmony.

Well, it strikes me that life, as we evolve and age, can be a small world; be aware of it, manage it, and embrace it, but don't be surprised by it. It can be good or bad, totally up to you, but more likely satisfying, if you go in eyes wide open.

Many of my friends, acquaintances, and clients have been world travelers and international businesspeople, and have a national or international network of friends, clients, and centers of influence challenged with industry trends, competitive pressures, and interaction with a myriad of personalities.

Should you transition from that to a lesser role or leave it altogether, it is very likely that your world will shrink dramatically. That could be completely by choice or necessity. It may be that your new purpose is caring for the health of a loved one or yourself. It may be a small community of close friends or a charity needing your help. It might be a grander stage to the service of God and country. If you have a choice, make an informed decision; if you don't have a choice, embrace it; savor the pace and contrast. Either way, at some point, your world will likely get smaller. Here is a nice quote from Dr. Seuss that may resonate: "To the world you are one person, to one person you may be the world."

Just like at Disney, you will find joy and peace knowing and living: "It's a small world after all."

———

Why make this harder than it needs to be? You have to decide and ultimately execute your plan for your future, sabbatical, retirement, or next chapter. You need to be honest with yourself and your partner, if you have one.

As I have said before, I am not the most religious guy, but that doesn't mean wey cannot take advice from religious texts. I like the Gospel of John 8:32;SJV : "The truth shall make you free." It seems to me if you get this right, you are free to enjoy your life to the max, not live in fear or uncertainty, and leave it better off for family and friends.

Even if you are not religious, we all need an advocate. Someone that is rooting for us, lifting us up, and contributing to our well-being, even when we haven't asked or don't even know it. The Gospel of John refers to the Holy Spirit as the Advocate that God sends when Jesus joins God after his death and resurrection.

That sure seems to me a good, logical reason to at least partially link our fulfillment with spirituality as a whole (no matter what you believe), and put a nice bow on a tangible financial and life plan and platform for eternal growth!

Physical

Perspiration and Perspective

I was reading about a queue of dozens of climbers waiting at thirty thousand feet of elevation to climb the last few feet to the summit of Mount Everest, the tallest peak in the world. At this height, oxygen depletes, naming it the death zone. This article didn't talk about how this happens and how these folks got here, but said you really have to know *why* they are putting themselves in this situation; what trumps everything is the drive and determination that have these folks not thinking about consequences but putting one foot in front of another at thirty thousand feet, where, in 1977, just two people made it. It may be a mission from a young age, it may be recovery from a near-death experience, it may be a traumatic event in their life, it may be the ultimate test of their fitness and mental toughness—whatever the reason, they are determined to do this.

Remember, or find, your *why*—your perspective is what this opportunity to advance/grow/retire means to you and no one else.

I have hiked a couple of sections of the Appalachian Trail in different states, and I've run into others like me and others with full gear, walking poles, and backpacks who are walking the same stretch on their way to completing their six-month excursion: covering twenty-two hundred miles and everything in between. We are walking on the very same path but with very different goals and outcomes, a little bit like life.

Continually seek, frame, and freshen your perspective, and apply a big dose of regular perspiration...and repeat.

Back to Your Roots

I learned and gained so much in nine days of driving one August in Wisconsin: eighteen hundred miles circling the state for the first time ever, even though I grew up and lived there most of my life. I had much to show for it, in addition to a sore back and no feeling in my legs. It was sunny and in the midseventies, with no humidity; there were open roads, as school was starting. I traveled from southeast Wisconsin, west to north, then east, and back to the south. Seventy-two counties, over five million people, and over ten thousand lakes populate Wisconsin, bordered by the largest river, and the Great Lakes...not that I got to all of these. This could be your state, your town, your car, your family, and your trip; you decide when you want to do this, and pick your geography.

I am always struck by the differences in culture, lifestyle, pace, and architecture. Earlier in the trek, I stopped at the home where my mother grew up. It was in a state of disrepair and neglect—to be expected after several generations, perhaps. Small towns, saloons, shrines to Christ and Mary popping out of landscape, reaching to the sky as an oasis and reminders of acceptance and peace, at our disposal, if we so choose.

Not all of those Wisconsin stereotypes are accurate, but I will just tell you, my week was like one big tailgate party. Beer, brats, cheese curds, lake whitefish (fried, preferably), a visit to the Packers' Lambeau Field, cruller donuts only found in Wisconsin, frozen custard, and did I mention, fish fries? I loved it all!

There was no one on the roads up north as I was doing 65 passing an Amish couple and horse and buggy going about 15 mph. With that big sign on the back side reading "Slow Down and Enjoy Life." Regular, reliable sightings and sounds of deer, bald eagles, loons, and so many others. My point? Clear your head, take your vacation, gain perspective, and see how others do it.

Many Right Turns: A Welcome Circle

If you know about basketball, leadership, and winners, you know about Marquette University in Milwaukee, Wisconsin, the national championship Marquette Warriors in 1977 coached by Al Maguire and Hank Raymonds. There was a one-man play about Al's life written by friend and cobroadcaster Dick Enberg. Maguire was a visionary, determined competitor, free spirit, and part showman who grew up in the Northeast. When he coached and lived in the Milwaukee area, he commuted to work, leaving his subdivision and turning left to Milwaukee's Marquette campus, often on his Harley-Davidson motorcycle (wearing no helmet) to go to practice and do what was expected of him. Some days he wouldn't, and I'm told you didn't know when or why, but his assistant coaches had to improvise. When someone asked Al where he was and why he didn't show up, he would simply reply, "Some days, you have to take a right turn and keep going." He would then take a road trip, have lunch or a beer with the locals, or just smell the roses and recharge his batteries. This worked for him. He was very unconventional; he didn't seem to care what others thought, and frankly, he had the coaches and team around him who respected him and his program. It energized him, his staff, and team and instilled a belief in themselves and the process that enabled them to sneak up on other teams and, according to many, outplay their skill set, beat better teams, and be crowned the best college basketball team in the country.

Take your share of right turns. You would be surprised how good it feels, how it helps you focus, how it emphasizes and develops your strengths, and instills belief in yourself for you and others. It shows how it makes you better at your left-turn destinations.

R&R: Not What You Think

I didn't really think Roundabout Rage was a thing. I had read a little bit about it in the past, but more and more I heard peers—and frankly, folks of all ages—talk about Roundabout Rage.

Maybe we have less patience, a stressful day, higher expectations, more people on the road with less experience and knowledge, or the newness of the road design concept. It could be the multiple lane roundabouts where you can see where you enter, but you're not sure if you will be exiting where you want without cutting off several fellow R&Rs. It could be GPS that tells you to take the third exit once you enter the roundabout, which is confusing because you're not sure if that gets you to the right place. It could be that the driver was paralyzed by fear, camping out at the entrance before they see no other cars at all, or incorrectly judging the speed of entry, especially while being distracted from the honking horns several cars back. It could be the unsure driver who is not clear where they are going, so they give you a dip and a head fake in each of the exit outlets. In theory, it is to save you time; it puts the onus on the faith and honor of each driver to accommodate increased volume. More thinking, less time, increased volume, and undereducated drivers are not a good combination.

In fact , in March 2020 an article appeared in the Wall Street Journal entitled " Roundabout Wrecks Have Engineers Going In Circles" written by Scott Calvert. It states the fender bender problem is the dirty little secret . There have been more than 6000 roundabouts in the country built since 1990 according to Oregon transportation engineering firm Kittleson and Associates Inc. .As one roundabout victim stated " Not everybody has the same attitude about what the rules are in these roundabouts".

One dear friend, while he experienced R&R, took matters into his own hands. He reached for the raw eggs he just picked up at the store and launched them through the open sunroof onto another car. It ended fine after apologies, a small fine, and an eggless recipe for dinner.

We're always learning life lessons from any situation: don't expect it to take less time if you want to proceed safely; hurrying rarely pays off, and it's a little thing. As someone once said, "Don't sweat the little things." But, just in case, always put the dairy and produce in the back seat, out of arms' way.

The Art of Doing Less

"Why You Should Embrace the Art of Doing Less": this headline was taken from the BBC newspaper, written by Svend Brinkmann, professor of psychology. For better or worse, I dip into the headlines and select articles in about ten or more papers or news websites in the morning (often finding nothing newsworthy, so generally, you are not missing anything).

I received one of those general emails with pithy, humorous insights into everyday life. Referencing the headline above, one quote that might fit that I recently heard is this: "When you ask me what I am doing today, and I say nothing, it doesn't mean I'm free; it means I am doing nothing."

The psychologist's point is that we are bombarded by social media and constant consumer marketing, being told we don't measure up. Someone is more successful and happier, and we are in constant need of something more in our material lives. He actually calls it the joy of missing out, adding that by accepting and embracing the limits in our life, we could actually feel happier and more fulfilled. He contends there is room for pleasure to disengage from the constant doubt of "Am I doing enough?" He cites Aristotle as one of the first to talk about a moderate life, striking a balance between doing way too much or too little.

Brinkmann says we are tempted every day and bombarded to do something more. He quotes the humor of Oscar Wilde, with Mr. Wilde saying that "he could resist everything, except temptation."

Take a moment, and don't lament what you are missing out on, but experience the joy of knowing you are doing what is most important for you and those in your life. Take these pieces and stories, and find a way to balance your stool.

SUMMARY AND ACTIVITY

Summary

- Embrace *disruption* and squash *destruction*.
- Your life and financial plans can be tools of well-being for you and those around you.
- In your life planning, embrace your mortality. Accept it, and find a way to make the most of your time on earth.
- The four legs of the balanced stool are spiritual, intellectual, physical, and social.

Activity

Break down the four legs of your stool by listing components that contribute to each of the four legs.

Honestly assess your ideal balance. Where you are today, and how you can address the gap over time?

How wobbly is your stool? How will you alter your life planning in order to address the wobble, so you don't fall over?

Advance through Life and Grow

You are never too old to set another goal or dream a new dream.
—C. S. Lewis

Healthy aging, no matter your current age, is the goal here: to improve and grow in all ways available to you at different stages. If you develop these traits of curiosity, self-awareness, and the pursuit of the balance that's right for you and your energy, you can persevere and thrive at almost any stage. Having said that, life happens: your health or the health of a loved one can direct your time and energy and redirect your efforts, as it should be, requiring you to adjust, reprioritize, and refocus. Work shouldn't be tedious or waiting on your ten years left on the job till retirement, if you are that unhappy.

Pursue your passion and purpose as a whole, or in segments. For example, take physical health—where can you compete, have fun, evolve, and learn—what are your strengths, and how do you leverage them? I was never going to be an NBA star, but there are some under six feet (which is in the zip code of my stature) who have done it. Friends, as a couple, are avid pickleball players, killing two birds with one stone, both the physical and social legs of the chair . They are the envy of the league, which consists of all ages.

Who can't learn more? The one warning here is it reminds me how much I don't know about so much. There are things to achieve here forever.

Your social circle will evolve with some and go deeper with others, and it is up to you, even through ups and downs, geography, and age differences.

There are many pinnacles in the spiritual world and disciplines, learning, degrees of peace, grace, and gratitude to be appreciated. I often need to be reminded to let life come at me and to not take things too seriously.

It hit me again the other day that when I spend time with our five grandkids ages six and under, I enjoy time with all of them, while also cherishing one-on-one time. I always ask them what they want to do, and invariably, whether alone or in a group, each will respond "I want to play, Papa."

We don't have to lose that altogether, and it is with us our whole lives, as you look back at the formative years. Look at trends in work, home, and school and the focus on making it fun, hands-on, and stimulating for adults of all ages in all those environments.

Retirement Place: Someday Isle (I'll)

I saved this excerpt of a poem by Dennis Waitley, a very accomplished writer and speaker and graduate of the US Naval Academy, that I heard someone, by memory, share with a group of financial advisors. It not only inspired them, but I am sure, as they shared it with clients, it inspired many to not only plan, but to also put into motion that plan, as "Someday I'll" is today!

"There is an island fantasy called "Someday I'll" we'll never see. Where Recession stops and inflation ceases, our mortgages are paid and our pay increases.

But happiness cannot be sought, it can't be sold and it can't be bought. For life's most important revelation, it's the journey that counts not just the destination.

Happiness is where you are right now, pushing your pencil or pushing your plow. It's going to school, it's standing in line, it's watching and waiting, it's tasting the wine. It's knocking on doors and making your calls; it's getting back up after your falls.

If you live in the past you become senile, if you live in the future, you're on Someday I'll. You can save and slave stretching mile after mile, but you'll never set foot on your Someday I'll.

For when you have paid in all of your dues, and put in all of your time. Out of nowhere comes another Mount Everest to climb. So, from this day forward make it your vow, to take Someday I'll and make it "NOW!"

To the Moon

I did a lot of reflecting on the fiftieth anniversary of the United States putting a man on the moon, about why and how that happened. Or maybe "to the moon" reminded you of that show *The Honeymooners*, when Ralph Kamden blustered about sending his wife, Alice, there when she rightfully called him out—"to the moon, Alice!" But I digress.

It's pretty remarkable what can happen when you set a vision and back it with resources, pure fortitude and determination, and a timeline. Also, the fact that we haven't done it since is a reminder that the rubber-band effect is always in play; we need to continue stretching and challenging and investing in ourselves, our passions, and relationships or there will be a diminishing effect.

With all the coverage on the fiftieth anniversary, I can't help but remember another astronaut, John Glenn, who dedicated his life to service. Of course, he was the first American to orbit the earth in 1962 three times and was brought down before seven orbits for safety reasons. I bring this up as I had forgotten that he was back up in space at age seventy-seven as a part of the *Discovery* space shuttle in 1998, and as a sitting senator. It actually served the Senate Committee on Aging's mission to determine the effects of aging physically and mentally, and what can be done to alleviate them. John Glenn served his country for nearly all of his ninety-five years, passing away recently in 2016.

Another real-time example is that of Admiral Ted Carter, introduced to me by a good friend, as a retired superintendent, the head of the US Naval Academy after forty-two years in naval service. He had graduated from the USNA and was one of the first highly decorated Top Gun aviators (before Tom Cruise!). Admiral Carter's words in the USNA publication were, "I am not *retired* retired"—another example of retirement being a misnomer. Look for him to reset and continue his life of service for many years to come.

Aging, learning, contributing, reinventing, and repurposing are all real things bringing real results. These things generally are a choice, your own path, your own way, and contribution—live it now; read about it later.

The Big Test

You may be working diligently on your big breakthrough: identifying it and making it happen. You may be wondering what you would do if faced with a crisis. It's great to be prepared and play out scenarios for the big test; because you are reading this and relating to it, you may very well be in good shape. Perhaps you had a big test before and would have liked to have done better.

As you think about it and want to enhance your chances, let me suggest you look for, recognize, and celebrate the everyday heroes. You may very well be one of them. Smaller tests of character, integrity, quick, effective judgment, and courage are all around you, and you may very well be an everyday hero or know one. Through day-to-day challenges to do the right thing at home, personally and professionally—the courage to take on a boss, coworker, or subordinate; the fortitude to do what you can do for your family, even when neighbors, family, and some friends disagree—you are your own everyday hero.

A dear friend of mine found himself in his fifties caring for his wife in her late forties with advancing Alzheimer's. He was surprised to talk to a number of caregivers and medical professionals who said many in his same situation would have left or relinquished the responsibility. Again, I cannot tell you what I or anyone else might or should do in those circumstances, but I *can* tell you that I and many others draw courage, strength, and hope, and witness a remarkable example of what one would do in a big test by this person's inspiring display as an everyday hero.

The everyday hero never asked for this, and this certainly was not in their plans for retirement. He would likely tell you, in many ways, without realizing it, he has been preparing his whole life to do the right thing and pass the big test by witnessing the everyday heroes in his life.

Forty Years to Find the Words

My awe and respect for the dedication, sacrifices, and courage of our military and their families grows with each interaction and each day. Growing up, as I have previously stated, it was something off in the distance, a war movie and some obscure references to my dad and uncles serving in different branches of service, but no details. A navy pea coat passed down from my uncle while I was in high school because it looked cool and he was going to give it away, and I still didn't connect the dots. Periodically, news reports questioned our government's motives and stories of a military war thousands of miles away.

My sophomore year in college, we welcomed a freshman roommate in our fraternity. We hung out, had a beer or two, and became fast friends, and to this day, he and his wife are among our dearest friends. He was a heck of a collegiate basketball player, holding many records today, and tells stories of his time with the pros. They are both dedicated advocates for our veterans and compassionate Gold Star family members, providing comfort and support for other Gold Star families all over the globe.

In all that time, I didn't know, and he didn't share until forty years later, that just before he came to college, he had lost his brother in Vietnam. People didn't talk about it or couldn't talk about it. Think about that—carrying that burden. Those emotions, subject to societal opinions…how in the world, and when, are you able to heal?

Thirteen of us, consisting primarily of my friend and his family, recently met for a familial Italian dinner, following a ceremony and tribute to veterans and naval aviators, featuring the very helicopter flown by many in the military: a refurbished Huey helicopter. The sound of the rotating blades of these helicopters was the sound of hope to those expecting food to be drop-shipped, or to be saved from enemy fire, or the wounded to be carried to safety. The helicopter piloted by my friend's brother, First Lieutenant Thomas Francis Shaw, a proud pilot of the 129th Army Air and Assault and Rescue Division, crashed on one of these missions. Both pilots died, and both side gunners were thrown out of the helicopter as they bravely defended their position, ignoring orders to strap in so they could position their guns and fire more effectively.

We listened intently and reverently as we heard of the circumstances surrounding this tragedy only because the soldier was just now, forty-five years later, able to talk about it. It was like a solemn moment in church, where one seeks answers and appeals to a Higher Power to make sense of things. Our soldiers need our help and support as they work through things, practice self-therapy, and get on with their lives.

A book written by Warrant Officer helicopter pilot Jim Crigler, the Vietnam tentmate of my dear friend's brother, Tom Shaw, called *Mission of Honor: A Moral Compass*, tells these stories and truly is an instrument of healing. After forty-five years, this book became the right words and the moral compass to guide one's life as well.

Your Money or Your Life?

Maybe your first thought is the old gangster movie where the robber threatens to kill the innocent bystander if they do not give the criminal their wallet. Or maybe you are ahead of the game and have read the book entitled *Your Money or Your Life*, by Vicky Robin, Joe Dominguez, and Monique Tilford, which is a good read and worthwhile.

The reality is that you may be robbing yourself of a complete and fulfilling life if you don't give some thought to financial life planning, and put something in motion that identifies your family's goals in all life stages, and decide how you will position money and resources to support that—not vice versa.

What prompted this stream of thought was a program my wife and I attended by Matthew Kelly, entitled *Passion and Purpose in Your Life*. Yes, he has written about and discusses the Christian way of life in many of his talks, but also does consulting for businesses and programs on leadership and building culture.

So, it was a Friday night from 7:00 to 10:00 p.m., and normally we would be doing anything but attending a program like this, and it struck me that there were five hundred to six hundred of us walking in, and we were of all ages. A number were retired, and many, by a show of hands, it appeared, were not. Would any one of us go out at that time for a program on financial literacy? Probably not, albeit they are inextricably linked.

The more we listened to Matthew Kelly,in his comments to us ,the more this resonated: "Anyone or anything that does not help you become the best version of yourself is too small for you." While you are working on your 401(k) deferral (which I highly recommend), are you working on the other part? While I expected to hear some Christian themes worked in, the points were broadly relevant and not, at first blush, of religious doctrine. You are reading this, but so what? What will you do about it? He would say, "Be present, right here, nowhere else; right now, never again."

Your engagement and ultimate success in journeying to your summit or a fulfilling life retirement are predicated on three things, according to Kelly:

1. Hungering for best practices
2. Continuous learning
3. Personal clarity

Even if you are agnostic, he would tell you that "who you become is infinitely more important than what you do, or what you have."

Put Success in Succession Plan

Having transitioned from a publicly traded company recently, and for the second time, there is a lot that goes into it for the person leaving and the people staying.

In my profession, I have worked with many owners who have been considering, or should be, planning for retirement and succession in their business. These go hand in hand when transitioning. By the way, it doesn't have to be all or nothing.

Retirement is multidimensional and often happens earlier than it did in the past. Most importantly, the key drivers are often the nonfinancial ingredients of a fulfilling advancement. Retirement doesn't have to mean downshifting or slowing down, just changing lanes. Turn traditional retirement on its head and advance!

An advisor would, of course, suggest doing the standard financial documents as you make your plans. Consider a personal action strategy session (PASS) of your own, which has a personal balance sheet highlighting the nonfinancial assets and liabilities, preparing you for a fulfilling advancement. For example, friends, family, causes, interests, exercising, part-time work, and faith. How many are in the plus column? What is your nonfinancial net worth, and are you positioned to advance or retreat?

Don't worry; as I alluded to, in the words of Bob Mowat, a longtime children's author, "Anything worth doing is worth doing poorly at first." You can change your mind and adjust along the way. Take time to personally decide what success looks like in transitioning for you, your business, and your family. What will it hurt to take a PASS at it?

Mind Your Own Business!

Do you have time off? Are you on sabbatical or between jobs or trying retirement? Are you more easily distracted, moving from one thing to another, not focusing on any one thing for too long? Likely, that's your newfound freedom, time to think and explore, with a fluid schedule and flexibility. That was not unlike you heading off to college or trade school after high school. You had plenty of time to evaluate, contribute, or wander. Zero in; if you're not sure, add education, credentials, give of yourself. It will help you pick a lane.

"If you live for people's acceptance, you will die by their rejection." This quote is attributed to the Grammy award-winning artist Lecrae. Steve Jobs said, "Don't let the noise of other's opinions drown out your own inner voice, and most important, have the courage to follow your heart and intuition."

I don't care what your age is; in these times of tweets, second-by-second news reports, twenty-four-seven countless channels with nothing on, and Facebook fantasy land, you can lose sight of what's important very easily. Acknowledge these times, these feelings; modify your behavior, and instill some order to an otherwise chaotic world, whatever your age.

I like a prayer for insight and will quote a portion here, "Days pass and the years vanish and we walk sightless among miracles. Lord, fill our eyes with seeing and our minds with knowing. How filled with awe this place and we did not know it" (Liturgical Press, *Celebrating the Eucharist*, 2019). Make the most of it, and mind your own business! Many others will be the grateful beneficiaries.

The Plane Truth

I typically bring reading material, grab an aisle seat, and hunker down for a relaxing, quiet plane ride. I will be polite but not encourage conversation. But recently, I bent most of my rules. A mother in her seventies and her daughter in her fifties were engaging; they were friendly real estate agents visiting family. They soon turned to me to bring me into the conversation. I took the bait, talking about our destination (where I live), and they were thinking of moving too. We had about forty-five minutes left of flying time.

I learned more about them in that time than I did with some colleagues in years. So we got to money, divorce, families, where to live, and when to move and retire.

Now, I try to have a rule that I don't say something about someone that I wouldn't say to a person's face, but I got chatty, and we were visiting like old friends. The mom said she won't or can't retire and doesn't see how anyone could enjoy that. She seemed type A with a need to work, and soon, in a nice way, said I should go find a job and get back to work, which I don't necessarily disagree with. We talked about making the most of one's physical and mental faculties until you lose them. I forgot how the voices of three animated people carry, even in those noisy planes. Apparently, the older couple in front kept glancing back at us.

I, have been working on judging others less and trying to understand or accept their views, if it doesn't affect anyone else negatively. Well, we got a little judgy of those who could enjoy the traditional definition of retirement, and not work for a paycheck, or seemingly, not have a purpose. I should remember that many can have a deep purpose and no paycheck, and that their plan and my plan can be worlds apart, and both be spot-on for each other.

So, since my plane mates were friendly and forthcoming, I asked them if they saw a connection between wealth and happiness. The mother said she knew a number of wealthy folks who weren't happy; of course, I asked why. She thought about it, and said those folks seem to not have a circle of good friends or family that they could trust. To which I referenced my writing about getting FOC'd. On the other hand, her happy, wealthy acquaintances had a cause and a purpose. So we imposed our views on the rest of the population and dismissed other views of aging as not good or appropriate.

We landed and were gathering our things to get off the plane. The couple in front turned around, annoyed. As we discussed entertainment in our destination city, they smugly said they have been retired for fifteen years from age fifty-five, living in the villages of Florida (which has a wild reputation for partying for those fifty-five and older). They said that before we knocked it, we should try that form of retirement! They were probably right, and they, and we, should not be annoyed or bothered by someone else's view of getting older and how one wants to spend that time and how unique an experience it can be.

The woman in front then politely talked about how they had a plan in their early fifties, built a home, and moved to the villages, and never looked back. They love it. That's awesome, and a good example that planning with a unified vision, and carrying it out with vigor and focus, can work well.

There are a few "plane" truths that came out of this exchange that one can apply. So fuel up, buckle up, take off, and navigate your plan—and enjoy the flight.

I Get More Done When I Have More to Do

Well, duh! Although most of us are busy, we like constant motion. It gives us a sense of action, accomplishment, and relevance—but are you productive, furthering your goals, making the most of your day and schedule, and aligned and balanced? Probably not, but that's OK. It's normal, but why be normal when you can be exceptional?

Believe me, I am not exceptional, but instead, a conflicted work in progress; I like routine, but I hate routine. I can fill a day, but I don't like to just fill my day.

There is power in traditions, discipline, positive habits, and setting the tone. Remember the legendary Green Bay Packers football coach Vince Lombardi, who said, "With discipline comes freedom." Freedom to win, to excel, to be your best, to open doors to grow and set new goals. Leave it to a world-class coach to say something that at first blush sounds like an oxymoron, but is so profound.

SUMMARY AND ACTIVITY

Summary
- "Someday Isle" (I'll) is today! Today and every day is the right time to make a plan and motivate yourself.
- Observe and appreciate yourself and the other everyday heroes around you and write them a handwritten note.
- It's not about retirement; it's about advancing and growing in the life you were given.
- After forty-five years, "Mission of Honor, A Moral Compass" are words to guide a life.
- Always be present in the right *now*.

Activity
Write down what *success* looks like for you and your family. How could you see yourself succeeding as a unit, and as individuals?

What do you need to do *now* in order to achieve this future success?

Where and how can you be your best, and what does it look like?

CHAPTER 6

Communicate, Listen, and Adapt

True humility is not thinking less of yourself;
it is thinking of yourself less.
—C. S. Lewis

This is a tough one for me. I get so involved with my agenda and too focused on checking the boxes. Communicating, listening, and adapting really take stopping the car altogether sometimes and not just trying to shift gears at 50 mph.

I read a reference in *Bloomberg News* (a respected source and tool for business) talking about the average married couple communicating with one another about twenty-seven minutes a week. Therein lies the challenge!

One of the oldest business books on my shelf is Stephen Covey's *Seven Habits of Highly Effective People*. Check it out if you haven't seen it lately.

Two things here that zero in for me are:

1. Listen first to understand.
2. Sharpen the saw.

Listen to yourself—honestly listen to yourself—and certainly listen to those you care about fully, before you prepare your response. Even after listening intently, playing it back, and being as sure as you can, and you might understand 60 percent! You can then understand the situation as fully as possible to determine your course of action, and adjust, and as Covey says, "sharpen the saw or further educate or adjust course."

As I mentioned earlier, you will likely not notice or change a lot consciously, but as you look back from future years, a lot certainly is different. The communication is the code you need to crack, or the lock that needs the key. Talking and communicating are two very different things.

I was getting the grandkids into the timeless eighty-year-old movie *The Wizard of Oz*. Remember when Dorothy first set out on the yellow brick road and she runs into the Scarecrow, who is convinced he needs a brain? She asks him how he can talk if he doesn't have a brain, to which he responds, "Some people without brains do an awful lot of talking, don't you think?"

He was wiser than he gave himself credit for, and, generally, so are we, but others around us won't know that unless we communicate well. Another notable read from a good friend is *The Four Agreements*, by Miguel Angel Ruiz, to help with understanding perspective, communicating and adapting.

1. Be impeccable with your word.
2. Don't take anything personally.
3. Don't make assumptions.
4. Always do your best.

So I admit I enjoyed researching a little bit of *The Wizard of Oz*, since I, too, have been watching it for decades; indulge me with one more thought on the importance of your mapping and living your life's journey and how to support that. A Scarecrow quote from the book: "For I consider brains far superior to money in every way. You may have noticed that if one has money without brains, he cannot use it to his advantage, but if one has brains without money they will allow him to live comfortably to the end of his days."

We all work hard to make the most of the brains we have. This take on it from L. Frank Baum is just a thought.

How Can I Stop Incessant Calls and Emails?
It's easy. Before I tell you, be careful what you ask for, and how quickly it will happen.

Some time ago, while working for a large organization and watching people come and go, I recall an executive announcing he was leaving. This is not uncommon in an acquisition or change in ownership structure. This executive announced that he was blown away by how quickly his phone and computer became quiet when he announced he was resigning.

When people perceive you as irrelevant, they may be briefly happy for you, and even a bit envious, but they move on to the new influencer.

My dad headed up the HR function for a large *Fortune* 500 company, and he used to say, "Don't leave a job unless you have a new job." That makes more and more sense. When you lose your platform, relevance, or current position, you are viewed differently—you are not a different person. I used to think it was a sign of disloyalty to explore your development and expand your horizons in the business community, that it would take away from your focus and effectiveness; in actuality, it helps. You owe it to yourself, and that perspective makes you a better employee.

So there are ways to handle, channel, and reduce the volume of incoming distractions; you may want to put in place those techniques before you make them go away altogether.

Build your platform of relevance continually, professionally, personally, and on multiple dimensions. Don't let someone else determine your relevance and focus. That sound of quiet can be deafening!

Think about Your Transition Plan before, as You Will Have a Lifetime to Think about It After

So they say we will be in driverless cars in five to ten years. Being the control freak I am, I'm not sure I will warm up to the idea. As you plan your transition to the next chapter or sabbatical, does it feel like you are driving the process or in the passenger seat of a clown car? I have seen it done many ways. It certainly depends a lot on your power to influence, owner or not, financial stake or not, your clarity and conviction on what you would like to do, and getting ahead of it and staying ahead of it, and leveraging your strengths and relevance in the business you are in.

Generally, be clear on what you want; consult those who can offer insight, confidentially, a partner or person your trust.

While it's nice to preserve and memorialize the past, what matters is how it will impact the company and people who remain after you leave. It's natural to think it won't be as good as if you were still there, but to insist that it will be, to those clients and employees. And the right successor or leadership will actually make sure it is, in fact, better.

Do your best to identify and influence the given outcomes; when it's time, communicate the vision and what it means to those remaining. Cherish and honor the past, and paint a picture of a compelling future—invest the time up front. I can almost guarantee you will have more than enough time on your hands to play it over again for time to come.

All That Glitters Is *Not* Gold

It may seem like the new, shiny object is to have total freedom and independence to do what you please every day, and it is, for a while. You can control your outlook, day, activities, and many of the outcomes. Just know it will be different; it took me a bit to realize it was not all about me, an affliction my wife will tell you I come about honestly, being the oldest of five with a stubborn streak that my determined Irish mother (God rest her soul) would attest to.

When working part time, I was present in someone else's space in my own home, my wife's office, and work area. I guess I might have offered a few suggestions on how things could be handled, yet didn't realize my view was not really solicited—and, oh, by the way, if I was going to get involved in the process at home, I better roll up my sleeves and help with chores.

Someone else had some expectations of me, and I didn't always appreciate them, know about them, or deliver on them. The need to communicate or realize these things became even more critical since we sold our home, moved twice, and were blessed with five wonderful grandchildren in the same five-year time span when all this was happening.

Don't get me wrong; I, and we, are so blessed and fortunate and wouldn't change a thing! But some of the glitter and gold is fool's gold that you need to sift through, not be taken in by the shine and get to the real thing, and enjoy the heck out of it. Once you get through the glitter, you will mine the main vein and get on with your treasured life and opportunity.

Not to worry. You can work through this and break through the other side with open communication, a mutual plan, and joint commitment to the solution, adjusting along the way. Get ahead of it, and don't waste time in empty mine shafts.

Enough about Me; What Do You *Think* about Me?

So, as you approach this stage of retirement, with decades of anticipation, liberation from all the have-to-dos and a growing intolerance for those who don't understand you (or drive as well as you do)—well, it has been described by a good friend as a honeymoon to start over and do whatever you want, except your partner may not feel they are part of this honeymoon.

Chances are while the retiring spouse feels completely free to pursue whatever they choose each day and is looking for a playmate, the other partner already has their own habits, routines, and plans—or this is, at least, what Katy tells me!

Not that we don't enjoy doing a number of things together, but we expect to adjust and communicate about it beforehand. It's a gift to get here, but it took me a bit to realize it was not all about me! I am told this is very common when a number of spouses I asked contributed to this informal poll.

Actually, these spouses are much better at speaking to this than I am, and when I asked Katy to write about this, she informed me she has other things on her agenda. Can you imagine?

Clothes Don't Make the Person...or Do They?

I recently listened to a speech by a military leader of Navy SEALs, Admiral McRaven, and he said every day, he started with neatly and completely making his bed; it set him on the right path for the day.

There is much discussion in corporations, businesses, and schools about dress codes. Can you tell me the difference between formal, business, casual, business casual, vacation casual, cocktail attire, or black-tie optional?

I could never bring myself to wear jeans on jeans day at work (probably because my jeans still look like they lived through the seventies, but I digress).

Let me relate three quick stories about very successful, multigenerational businesses' views on the matter.

Third- and fourth-generation businesses are rare, as often the founder's purpose and passion and products diminish or disappear over time. In each of these three cases, it was standard and expected to have managers wear coats and ties to work, meeting with clients and prospective clients.

There are many reasons to abandon this policy. As these businesses were in the manufacturing space, the age of the management team was in their thirties and forties, and in another instance, in their sixties and seventies, and believe it or not, in the eighties and nineties, and even got to be one hundred years of age. There are lots of reasons to break rank and go casual—I've earned it; no one in their forties wears suits, or it cramps their style—but they stuck with it. The reality is that these three businesses were thriving and evolving, with character and continuity for multiple generations, and they saw themselves committed to this with a plan and determination for generations to come.

So, it may be a small thing, and I know the clothes don't make the person, but did the clothes come first, or their success?

Most Divorces Are Due to Money

It's not about the money...it's about the money! But is it? Think about it.

You've heard the statistics and undoubtedly had conversations of your own about money that didn't go as you thought they would. If money issues cause stress, in general, and the divorce rate for those over sixty years of age is on the rise and higher than it is for younger couples, is it really about the money?

I would suggest it is not that simple. Consider it's about your life's journey; the choices you make, the goals you have or don't have, the events in your life (planned and unplanned), how prepared you are, and how you respond to adversity and surprises. As a self-diagnosed work in progress, I don't say this lightly.

Take a moment to understand your background and perspective on money by examining how you were raised, what your parents' perspective on money was, and thus, how you were influenced.

There are a lot of events throughout life that involve money, from school, to lifestyle, weddings, home, entertainment, family, and the big one waiting for all of us: retirement.

How do you handle those many money choices along the way, and to what extent will they influence retirement? Please note that your basis for those decisions and your satisfaction is predicated on how you handle, prepare, and carry out your life's journey, dreams, and reality, and communicate with a partner or others who are impacted.

It's not too big of a stretch, nor am I suggesting you get too worked up about it, but simply to connect the dots between your upbringing, values, risk profile, hopes and dreams, your money choices, and certainly your fulfillment, as you grow in life and approach retirement.

It can be perhaps surprising to many, by suggesting preparation for a fulfilling retirement begins well before age sixty and perhaps in your twenties and thirties and forties.

You Could Become This Person

Here's a little diversion to highlight the importance of expectations as you approach retirement. You could find yourself:

- bringing your loose change to McDonald's and ordering the senior coffee (i.e., legal money laundering)
- going to the grocery store in the middle of the day, seeing that everyone else looks like they just woke up and did the same thing
- seeing it's too much work to change clothes for three days
- avoiding rush hour at all costs, which is three hours in the morning and three hours in the afternoon
- with people opening the door for you, speaking more slowly and loudly to you, and asking if you are familiar with email
- thinking scheduling one big thing a day is plenty
- having a reunion with your buddies every time you go to the doctor's office
- having to explain that retirement does not mean dormancy or death
- debating with friends regarding who has the best antidepressants and other meds

"Spirit, are these the things of the future that might be or the things that will be?" said Scrooge to the Ghost of Christmas Future...a good sentiment as you process and prepare ; from Charles Dickens , A Christmas Carol.

SUMMARY AND ACTIVITY

Summary

- The average married couple actually communicates approximately twenty-seven minutes a week.
- Take a moment to understand your background and perspective on money, and how it could be affecting your current situation.
- Think about your transition plan now—because you will have a lifetime to think about it later.

Activity

If you have a partner, write down what you believe your partner's goals are for a fulfilling life and discuss with them. If you don't, readdress your written goals from past activities, and see if they have changed.

Take these discussion points, and find a common ground with your partner or with yourself.

CHAPTER 7

Scorecard, Resources, and Next Steps

You have access to the tools, the knowledge with which to take steps forward and put things in a higher gear toward defining and reaching your goals.

The guidelines are there, the standard set; the boundaries, limits, and urgency are up to you. As you need more information and feedback, it is out there on any subject. You should be cautious in your search, for the same reason you don't play doctor by analyzing symptoms and coming to conclusions on the internet.

If you need help getting started, taking it to the next level, jumpstarting your *why*, and zeroing in on your joint personal and professional goals, please contact me. If I can't help, I'm hopeful, or perhaps I can put you in touch with someone who can.

Here are a few final resources and advice. All the best on your journey to your summit!

Are You Successful?

Only you can answer if you are on the road to success. You define it, you own it, and you deliver on it. It's hard to get there and know that you are gaining on it, if you don't know what it looks like for you. The following are two different ways and sources for defining it:

Ralph Waldo Emerson:

To laugh often and much; to win the respect of intelligent people and the affection of children, to earn the appreciation of honest critics and endure the betrayal of false friends, to appreciate beauty, to find the best in others, to leave the world a bit better, whether by a healthy child, a garden path, or a redeemed social condition; to know even one life has breathed easier because you lived. This is to succeed.

Nadine Stair, age eighty-five, a woman from Louisville, Kentucky

If I had my life to live over again, I'd dare to make more mistakes. I'd relax, I would limber up...I would take more chances...I would eat more ice cream and less beans. You see, I'm one of those people who live sensibly and sanely hour after hour, day after day. Oh, I have had my moments and if I had it to do over again, I'd have more of them. In fact, I'd try to have nothing else. Just moments, one after another, instead of living so many years ahead of each day. I have been one of those persons who never goes anywhere without a thermometer, a hot water bottle, a raincoat and a parachute. If I had it to do again, I'd travel lighter. I would start barefoot earlier in the Spring and stay that way later in the Fall. I would go to more dances. I would ride more merry-go-rounds. I would pick more daisies.

The Art of Giving Back

I learned about giving the hard way. When I started in banking a few years back, I was welcomed on my first day, filled out normal paperwork, and given a charity pledge card and encouraged to consider a gift. Being a tad stubborn, I resisted and then gave a small amount through payroll deduction. Slowly, I learned a lot about this organization, saw firsthand the benefits, and got involved, ultimately giving to that charity each year I worked.

I have been fortunate to work in an industry that encourages its associates to volunteer and support many community and charitable causes. It may seem self-serving at first, but if it is, you won't last long or do very well at it.

Sometimes, giving of your resources is not easily measured in the short run, and not always clearly connected to the end result. In fact, it is more of a reflection on whom we hire, why they want to work with us, how we take care of our clients, and how we work together and grow as a team of professionals and individuals.

When a dear friend sent me the commencement speech given by Anna Quindlen, a Pulitzer Prize–winning author, Villanova, it struck me that she said, "I no longer consider myself as the center of the universe…we are all still students learning how to best treasure our connection to others…love is not leisure, it is work."

The work of art is very much a work in progress, but we like how it is taking shape.

PASS: Personal Action Strategy Session

This is a comprehensive process and series to jump start or adjust course along the way. Following are the key ingredients of the recipe—how much time, energy, and focus are a function of where you are at and whether you are tackling this yourself or with some guidance:

- Definition of success
- Pitfalls of traditional retirement
- Advancement (Who needs retirement?)
- Your life purpose; a personal vision statement
- Roadblocks to happiness
- Resources to guide you

Current state: Evaluate on scale from 1–10 (highest) whether the following are assets or liabilities, contribute to or detract from your well-being, and tally net impact today.

- Family, friends, work, hobbies, faith, health, financial, other.

Future state: Do the same for what you would like it to be and tally.

Assess gap, and put in place a plan to improve your personal assessment net worth, and let's review quarterly. Do an annual comprehensive assessment factoring in changes in life, status, and attitudes. Review, adjust, and renew.

Scorecard When the Game Changes

Not sure where you are going, but making good time? Going from many meetings, metrics, profit and loss statements, performance indicators, business plans, and W-2s to none of that is strange. I am suggesting that your scorecard morph a bit so you know you are making the most of your talents in a new direction, so you may be productive and contributing day in and day out, looking back with a sense of accomplishment and pride.

I have talked about a personal balance sheet, highlighting your personal traits, strengths, investments in yourself, and any liabilities or detractors to your health and well-being. That's one way of scoring progress.

Next, map out redefined goals (e.g., travel national parks, work community service hours, earn a part-time income, schedule your family time and events, find books to read, implement exercise regimen, or find courses to take and degrees to earn).

It's there, it's doable, and it's up to you to put structure in place. No one is saying you have to do this; it's your call. You could have as much time in advancement as you had in your career; put a plan in place so you look back on this period one, five, ten, or twenty-five years from now with a sense of fulfillment.

What a gift and a blessing: new worlds to discover; people to influence; things to learn; a chance to open your eyes, slow down, or gear up to see the awesome world around you every day!

Planning without Discipline

Many of us are not the best at following the rules, doing what we are told, or taking someone else's suggestion as gospel.

We might be determined, curious, and reasonably intelligent and envision a plan for the future, but we are not disciplines enough or clear on how to execute it. It's OK; admit it and do something about it. But why?

For that answer, I again refer to a quote by the legendary pro football coach, Vince Lombardi: "With discipline comes freedom." His players did not like his regimen, a relentless pursuit of perfection and conditioning, but they found they won championships. Many of the same players were on losing teams before playing for Vince.

When you win and reach your goals, it's the most liberating feeling. It gives you the freedom or platform to do what you want, with whom, and when. It can take you to new levels, a higher purpose, and a deeper state of satisfaction and confidence.

So don't take my word for it, but isn't that what most of us seek: financial freedom and independence? Let me know if you would like help on that discipline thing—from one stubborn person to another. In fact, George Kinder defines Life Planning as "the most efficient process for delivering freedom into a persons life."

So...What's Next?

It's your move; what will be your next step? You've been thinking about it for a while, and maybe you received a nudge from this material. Take a step, tell someone, and begin or continue the process at the beginner level, or all the way to the expert level.

We know it's about lifelong learning, and if you are not learning more every day, then you are forgetting. Who wants to say they are getting dumber every day?

Have a conversation with yourself, a friend, your partner, a respected colleague, or relative. Talk about what you want to accomplish, get a view from someone else that you are on the right track, and put it in motion.

Identify local resources or specialists upon whom you might draw as you progress; this might be a therapist, an accountant, insurance professional, attorney, local banker, financial planner, or life coach. With this on your radar, you may begin to hear things about them, getting a referral or an introduction. Remember, you're in charge. No one gets into your inner circle without your permission and approval—somewhat like finding a good doctor or mechanic before you really need one.

Make it real, and write your next steps down. Put it where you can see it every day, and do what you say with a timeline. Regularly review it for progress, feedback, accuracy, and revisions. You and this journey are anything but static or stable. Don't let yourself off the hook. When you do it, celebrate and set new objectives. It may be little things, like a special coffee or a night out, dinner, or a trip. You and your trusted circle are your biggest supporters. Clear your head, and take a breath. I'm guessing you put enough pressure on yourself, more than others put on you, so recognize when you are progressing.

SUMMARY AND ACTIVITY

Summary

I'm closing with a family mission statement that is a work in progress, which I have shared with my family. It acts as a guide or, in some ways, at different stages, hopefully a road map for accountability, consistency, and fulfillment/success.

For those who may be looking more specifically at how they might approach retirement, you will find a formula and this tool to ideally enhance your preparation and your experience.

Later in this section, I have included excerpts from past comments that were in response to what the organizers told me they wanted to hear. I hope it provides some helpful background and perspective.

Activity

Family Mission Statement

What are your guiding principles for a family mission statement? Check the boxes as you create your own version of these ideas!

_____Put in relentless hard work and purposeful execution.

_____Believe in and support and encourage each other.

_____Think big about what each can contribute and accomplish.

_____Acknowledge a responsibility to make the most of good fortune, blessings, and skills.

_____Embrace challenges and adversity, and know you can rise above them.

_____Manage risks and rewards—a proven formula for success.

_____When you fail or fall short, retool, reload, and aim high again.

_____Treat others with respect and live with integrity.

_____Cherish the past, and challenge the future; build a legacy.

_____Embrace our individual differences and optimize them.

_____Realize that the whole is greater than the sum of the parts.

_____Each day is a gift; approach it with gratitude.

_____Hold yourself and each other accountable with open, honest dialogue.

_____Care less what others think.

_____Form opinions based on fact and firsthand observations.

_____Know that what you have to say is important.

_____Listen to understand before speaking.

_____Live every day with one eye on the future, making good choices.

_____Give yourself a break; don't be too hard on yourself and keep guilt in check.

_____Find some faith, nurture it, and draw peace and joy from it.

_____Be guided by your inner compass, not external social media direction.

_____Protect these treasures.

_____Celebrate success.

_____Realize that this is dynamic; create it, improve it, own it.

Assessment Tool: Retirement Ready, or Work to Do?

Rate the following statements on a scale of 1 (Poor) to 5 (Best)

_____You have a clear plan for succession in your company.

_____If yes, it is completely clear to all those that need to know and will be affected.

_____You have sufficient financial resources to leave your job, voluntarily or otherwise.

_____You have a clear plan for your days when this sabbatical or retirement begins.

_____You are leaving a job where you have a sense of accomplishment; and if so, you have a strong scorecard in the future.

_____If you have a partner in your business and/or at home, they answer the questions similarly.

_____You have looked at what your income will look like the next twenty-five years after your W-2 goes away.

_____You are working hard now to save for something twenty-five years out.

_____You and your family worked and invested to build a business with a plan to optimize its value in the future.

_____You are doing now what you thought you would be, and you are loving it.

So if you didn't score a 5 on each of these, where do you start to get on track?

- Enhancing Financial literacy?
- Crystallizing a shared vision with your partner?
- Bringing that vision to life?
- Finding the right people to run my business?
- What and how do I communicate this?
- Will we have resources to do what we want?
- Should I begin developing my new scorecard?
- Am I working for money or having money work for me?

SAMPLES OF PAST COMMENTS AND INSIGHTS

Community Leader of the Year Award: United Way
I was privileged to receive the Community Leader of the Year Award at United Way. Following are my comments, as it provides a bit of insight into why/how I do what I do. It's one example as you evaluate others' approaches and motivation.

Congratulations to all the recipients today; thank you to the United Way nominating and selection committees and to each of you for being here today, and for all you do for our community!

I am very honored, humbled, and frankly more than a bit uncomfortable. United Way said a good talk would be about 15 minutes, I said a great talk would be about 5 minutes, so can we go from good to great? We will see…

I don't feel any wiser on my birthday today, in fact, I am very much a work in progress, but please allow me to share a few thoughts that mean something to me and hopefully to you.

I enjoy, and am grateful for my life, but actually, it is not that interesting. It is more interesting and fulfilling to focus on others, and help where you can. Learning of other's stories, plans and challenges, and trying to help. It's energizing!

A very good friend just sent me Anna Quindlen's (a Pulitzer Prize–winning author) commencement speech at Villanova. She says, "I no longer consider myself as the center of the universe, we are all still students, learning how to best treasure our connection to others, love is not leisure, it is work." For those of us here, it is what we do and we feed off each other; maybe someone said you should, maybe it feels good, maybe someone helped you, it has become second nature. But for many it is not.

It is about the Forrest Gump effect…if you saw the movie, he didn't let anyone tell him what he can't do, he didn't always have a plan, (he just started running, playing Ping-Pong, football and shrimping), but he got out and took some risks with a simple core value system, work ethic and it worked, he accomplished a great deal, he found himself with some amazing people, and very compelling surroundings, and to be very fortunate and grateful.

Go see how someone else does it, learn and come back and apply it. Katy and I and our three daughters, Sara, Annie, and Kelsey moved to Columbus, Ohio in 1992, and were there nearly 15 years. Great city, but they were debating and struggling with how to fund the arts, having nothing like the United Performing Arts fund in Milwaukee, watching organizations falter and fail while they debated to unify. When we moved back, you realize how special it is here, you can influence things and there is no point in waiting for someone else to do something.

On that point, never underestimate or forget about the power of your asking someone to help. Please ask someone new to get involved, you will be surprised.

Quick story: Katy and I were fortunate to be in California on a trip with Carroll University, riding in a car with Andrea and Tony Bryant, talking about the giving community (if you know the Bryants, there is no one more generous) and observed that when moving back, we found many of the same people leading the giving in the community. I asked Tony who are the people in the next generation that need to provide leadership. Tony looked at me and said, Iit's you, Dave and Katy." We got called out very nicely and we took that to heart.

Get started; many of you get started giving back in grade school and high school. Carroll engages their students by swiping meal cards for United Way, and I know many of you are engaging young people early, forming those habits and that's tremendous!

Create a culture; when I started at First National Bank of Waukesha, I filled out the application and am grateful to Lee Melville, the president at the time who told me about United Way, and suggested I consider supporting it and why.

Initially, often, one does it because someone else thinks it is a good idea, then you'll learn more, internalize, and engage. I am grateful to First Business Bank, our holding company CEO, Corey Chambas, Milwaukee bank chair John Silseth and our entire team for the culture of community, sense of larger purpose, and encouraging one another to make an impact; and am especially grateful to J.P. Morgan colleague and dear friends Dave and Camille Kundert for believing in me more than I believed in myself and supporting us all along the way.

Our mission is larger than any one of us, but that one small thing you do, the vision you have, the purpose you feel, can be multiplied by forming alliances; find people, organizations that share your passion, a sense of urgency, and action orientation. For me, I am fortunate to know Carroll University, Waukesha County Manufacturing Alliance, Waukesha County Community Foundation, GPS Education Partners, United Way, United Performing Arts Fund and a number of others over the years in southeast Wisconsin.

Join forces, share resources and make a difference. Recapping:

1. More fulfilling focusing on others
2. Love is not leisure, it is work
3. Forrest Gump effect

4. See how it is done elsewhere
5. Please ask someone new to help
6. Create the culture
7. The multiplier effect—form alliances

Finally, in addition to my parents, Jim and Carol Vetta, my siblings, our children Sara, Annie, and Kelsey and their spouses and our grandchildren and our close friends, I need to recognize my volunteer of the year for the last three decades who without her encouragement, gentle nudges and accountability, and love and support, I wouldn't be here. So, thank you all and join me in recognizing my United Way campaign co-chair, my wife, Katy!

Don Richards Leadership Award

I'd like to recognize and thank the Don Richards family, the Milwaukee Business Journal and the work that the Waukesha County business alliance is doing and I'm very privileged that I've actually interacted with in one way or another for charitable work or business each of the prior award winners. So knowing them personally is very humbling and a significant honor, and I need to tell you how grateful I am…and how old I am!

My family has deep roots here in Waukesha; my dad's folks came over from Italy. My grandfather ran the little shoe repair store. My mom and dad raised five kids in the Waukesha and Milwaukee area and Dad worked his way up to an executive at Square D and we still have a number of relatives spread throughout the area.

Simply couldn't do it without my wife, life partner and best friend, Katy, and the family support of our daughters Sara, Annie, and Kelsey and their husbands and our five grandkids with whom we will be spending more time, as well as the culture within First Business that enables me and our team to give back and contribute in a meaningful way in the Waukesha/Milwaukee region.

Finally, today may be a little bit about a few people's stories, but every day, everyone here has their story, what they are doing to make this a better place. I have to tell you about one man's story, where he overcame life-threatening Guillain-Barré in his 20s, worked to build a 60+ year family business for multiple generations with his father; he coaches and contributes, raised three wonderful kids with his beautiful wife and today cares for his wife Toni who is consumed with Alzheimer's. Dr. Dean Copoulos is truly a hero and a leader! Let's remember Dr. Dean and all of those daily heroes and leaders and let them know how much they mean to us and our community!

So I appreciate the opportunity you have given me to look back and reflect; each of you is about leadership, and leadership is about looking forward. And I am most excited and heartened by the vision you have for this region, the future has never been brighter, and the time is now! Let's go do it!

EPILOGUE

I am a little embarrassed that I started this project with observations, notes, and conversations from over thirty years ago. However, it's not any less relevant. It is a platform to learn, observe, write, and memorialize; such as a photographer might, as they see how they evolve in thought and works by looking at their pictures over time, or, if I may, a budding artist with their canvases.

It is a tool for introspection—sparking idea or action from a reader, or maybe a conduit from which to learn. You are a connector to those that want to share and explore these ideas. You can challenge and continue growing yourself and support increased financial literacy for a life well lived.

This book is a small way of showing my gratitude and respect, and to acknowledge the many people who have had a profound effect on my life, enriching it in so many ways. There are so many dimensions or layers to each of our lives. I hope to explore those, learn from those, and develop them with your help—and also, perhaps our paths cross where we can learn from and develop together in person. It's hopefully a way to connect some hopes and dreams with those that can make them happen. Good things happen when you're bringing good people together. The power of you, the technology of today, and a clear sense of what's possible can change your life and mine.

REFERENCES AND RESOURCES

Following are sources for this book and other possible resources for you

Anthony, Mitch. *The New Retirementality: Life Centered Planning and Return on Life. Wiley 2020*

Baum, L. Frank. *The Wizard of Oz.*

Bloomberg News

BBC. "The Art of Doing Less," Svend Brinkmann, professor of psychology

Brooks, David. *The Second Mountain , Random House , 2019*

Carroll University Wisconsin , Financial Literacy , analytics and discipline focus

Catholic World Report, September 25, 2012

Center for Financial Planning

Copoulos, Dr. Dean. Distinguished entrepreneurial dentist, coach, champion athlete, and contributor.

Cotton, Tom, "Sacred Duty", William Morrow, 2019

Covey, Stephen. The Seven Habits of Highly Effective P*eople, Simon and Schuster , 2012 edition*

Crigler, Jim. Author , *Mission of Honor:A Moral Compass For a Moral Dilemma* , Panoma Press , 2017, entrepreneur, Gold Star Family champion and heroic Vietnam combat veteran.

Danko, William, and Thomas Stanley. *The Millionaire Next Door.*1996

Debbink, Admiral Dirk. Entrepreneur, past head of Naval Reserves, USNA, distinguished philanthropist. Admiral Ted Carter, past superintendent, US Naval Academy, and Top Gun aviator.

Dickens, Charles. *A Christmas Carol ; Chapman and Hall 1843*

Dominguez, Joe, and Vicki Robin. *Your Money or Your Life.* Penguin 2008

Eisenberg, Lee. *The Number* , Simon and Schuster 2006

Emerson, Ralph Waldo. Definition of success. 1841 , several volumes

Dick Enberg's *The Life of Al McGuire.a one act play* , 2005

Ferencz, Benjamin, benferencz.org for history, books and more

Gladwell, Malcolm.prolific author *Outlier Effect, Talking to Strangers, Tipping Point* and others through a myriad of publishers over 2 decades

Graham, Benjamin. Intelligent Investor.Harper and Brothers , 4th edition 1973

Gold Star Families and related organizations at the federal and state levels

Goodwin, Rob. Retired naval commander and aviator, and contributor, IT executive, philanthropist.

Hay, Tina, "Napkin Finance, A Visual Guide To Money", Dey Street Books, 2019

Jendusa, Jerry, Paul Schulls, and Jim Harasha. *Get Unstuck , Strategies to Move Your Business 2017; STUCK advisory services*

Journal of Financial Planning

Journal of Financial Therapy-

$Jumpstart Coalition

Just, Jerry. Health sciences entrepreneur, record setting athlete

Kelly, Matthew. *Principal of, A Dynamic Catholic,* entrepreneur and accomplished author

Kinder, George. *Institute of Life Planning.*

Kundert, Dave and Camille. Retired Chairman JP Morgan Asset Management: *Little Blue Book of Management Principles*, veteran and philanthropist. "when you reflect on significant achievements you always find a level of exemplary teamwork that has driven it."

Lewis, C. S. Historian, accomplished author on Christianity. *Mere Christianity* and *The Chronicles of Narnia*, poetry, and history. Many books in 1940's and 1950's

Lowry, Erin. Broke Millennial: Stop scraping by and get your financial life together, TarcherPerigree , 2017

Lynham, Doug. *Monk to Money Manager.* Thomas Nelson , 2019

Mauthe, Jean and Joe , contributors , CEO of a not for profit organization providing services to those in need of shelter.

McCloy, Mara. Talented editor from the College of Charleston.

Miller, Steve. Insurance executive entrepreneur, distinguished
    athlete, community citizen, and contributor.
Moncher, Tim. Insurance entrepreneur, hall of fame athlete,
    contributor. Don Moncher, good man, everyday hero.
National Financial Educators Council
Orman, Suze. *The Nine Steps To Financial Freedom: Practical
    And Spiritual Steps So You Can Stop Worrying.; prolific
    author from 1997 - 2020*
Ramsey, Dave. *Total Money Makeover , prolific author from
    1992 -2020*
Sanduski, Steve, Belay Advisors and Mitch Anthony partners
    -Return On Life
Shaw, Dave. Investment professional, hall of fame All-
    American athlete, and Gold Star family member.
Siegel, Cary. *99 personal money management principles to live by.*
Sinek, Simon. *Start with Why.Penguin , 2009*
Sunstein, Cass, and Richard Thaler. *Nudge : Improving
    Decisions About Health , Wealth and Happiness ,
    Penguin , 2009*
Thaler, Richard. *Advances in Behavioral Finance, Russell Sage
    Foundation , 1993*
Vetta, Katy. Wonderful partner and mother, accomplished author.
Vetta, Tom. CFO , CPA , champion athlete
Waitley, Dennis. *Someday Isle, a prolific author , many books
    from 1979 into the 21st century, aviator/graduate United
    States Naval Academy*
Warfighter Advance in Maryland, advancing the healing of
    our military heroes

Williamson, Marianne. , A Return To Love , Harper One , 1996 , *What's Your Deepest Fear.*

Zientarski, Sue, Jean Mauthe, Patty Sullivan , Tom Vetta and their families ; the best ever .

Speaking and Seminar Topics

- Do bankers have a soul, and how do you find it?
- What you need to know about your bank
- Where life planning and financial literacy intersect as they are inextricably linked
- Where do spirituality and discipline come into play?
- Leadership, from ground level to the stage; work life and attending the Leadership Institute at the US Naval Academy-through the eyes of friends- graduate and speaker ; and a successful entrepreneur in attendance
- Does accidental volunteering count?
- Networking for the introverted and liking it
- Book topics and discussions

ABOUT THE AUTHOR

 Born in Waukesha, Wisconsin, Dave Vetta was educated at Whitefish Bay, Carroll College, and University of Wisconsin, with advanced studies at Northwestern University and the University of Virginia Darden School of Business, receiving his MBA and certified financial planner designation. He has been recognized with community and athletic Hall of Fame honors at Carroll University, and by his peers for professional and community achievement.

Dave, his wife, Katy, and their family have roots in Wisconsin and Illinois, with time spent in Columbus, Ohio. They now spend time near Charleston, South Carolina, and Annapolis, Maryland, enjoying their three daughters and their husbands, and their five grandchildren whenever they can.

Dave has four siblings and had a loving upbringing, and has spent much of his professional career in many aspects of banking and investments in one of the largest banks in the country, and a niche business bank.

He believes that adding credentials along the way complements the professional experience and enhances one's perspective and fulfillment, all the while trying to be sensitive to the many good folks he encounters as friends, clients, and community leaders, and doing what he might, in some small way, to contribute to their well-being, as they most certainly contributed to his, for which he will be forever grateful.

He would love to hear from you, get your feedback, and hear your experiences to help promote financial literacy and enrich life's journey for others. The more we can do to facilitate each individual's fulfillment through clarifying goals, fueling their passion, and realizing their dreams, the more we win! Be well!

Contact

Connect on LinkedIn

Reviews, testimonials, and more stories are

appreciated at dvetta@aol.com

journeytoyoursummit.com

CPSIA information can be obtained
at www.ICGtesting.com
Printed in the USA
LVHW022310270520
656772LV00019B/3283